To: R. Grenville Patterson
From: Mom   2004 Christmas

MW01179032

Gone to Yacht:
A Pictorial History of Sailing on the St. John River

by

Herman Sullivan M.D.

DREAMCATCHER PUBLISHING
Saint John • New Brunswick • Canada

Copyright © 2004 Herman Sullivan

First Printing - July 2004

All rights reserved. No part of this publication may be reproduced or transmitted in any form or by any means - electronic or mechanical, including photocopying, recording or any information storage and retrieval system - without written permission from the Publisher, except by a reviewer who wishes to quote brief passages for inclusion in a review.

DreamCatcher Publishing acknowledges the support of the New Brunswick Arts Council.

Canadian Cataloguing in Publication Data

Sullivan, Herman - 1929

Gone to Yacht

ISBN - 1-894372-44-1
    1. Royal Kennebecasis Yacht Club--History. 2. Yachting--New Brunswick--Saint John--History. I. Title.

    GV823.R635 S85 2004   797.1'246'06071532   C2004-904516-4

Editor: Catherine Thompson

Typesetter: Chas Goguen

Cover Design: Dawn Drew, INK Graphic Design Services Corp.

Printed and bound in Canada

DREAMCATCHER PUBLISHING INC.
105 Prince William Street
Saint John, New Brunswick, Canada E2L 2B2
www.dreamcatcherbooks.ca

Grandmother, when asked the whereabouts of her boys,
replied, "They have gone to yacht."

TABLE OF CONTENTS

The Royal Kennebeccasis Yacht Club

At A Glance

1894	Saint John Yacht Club formed with anchorage for six yachts at Indiantown.
1895	Anchorage moved to Millidgeville and first Clubhouse erected.
1898	Application made for Royal Warrant and name changed to Kennebecasis Yacht Club. Royal Warrant granted by Queen Victoria, but due to spelling error in "Kennebecasis", the Club became the Royal Kennebeccasis Yacht Club.
1899	Admiralty Warrant granted - each yacht had the right to wear the Blue Ensign of her Majesty's fleet, *The Blue Duster*.
1901	Second Clubhouse built at a cost of $3,000.
1902	Club badge and burgee registered with the Department of Agriculture.
1923	Women gained Junior Membership status.
1925	Powerboat committee formed.
1926	Electricity installed in the club Railway committee formed.
1931	First Annual Endurance race was held.
1953	Main wharf constructed.
1956-58	Marine Railway constructed.
1964	Junior Sailing program began.
1970	Causeway, breakwater and dockside berthing added.
1978	Steel spar shed built.
1989-90	Clubhouse renovated, new fixtures and yard improvements cost more than $750,000.
2002	Membership elected first female Commodore.

Saint John is almost surrounded by water and has been associated with sea and the St. John River since its existence. Few accounts of recreational sailing in the area have been published. *Rags and Strings*, printed by the archives committee of the Royal Kennebecasis Yacht Club, is relatively recent, created in 1986. This current effort is possibly more pictorial and anecdotal but may serve as a companion to the other book.

Saint John, looking south from the Kennebecasis

Northern Saint John and Millidgeville, looking west

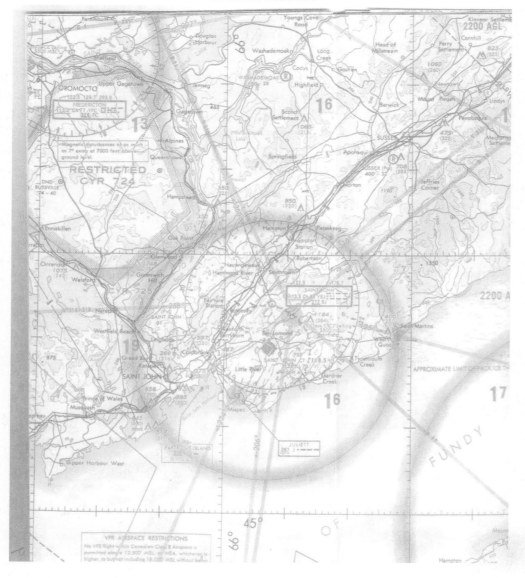

Airport chart, local area – communications boundaries
courtesy Ministry of Transport, charts & navigation services

OLD TIMES

The Greenhead limestone formations near the mouth of the St. John River are said to be some of the oldest in the world, dating back seven hundred and fifty years. There have been major alterations in geology since, with Africa abutting New Brunswick and separating to form the Atlantic Ocean. The last ice age went on until about ten thousand years ago. Man lived in North America by that time. The St. John River is thought to have emptied into the Bay of Fundy through South Bay and Drury Cove before the Narrows were "blasted" open, probably by earthquake or tectonic shift. The native peoples attributed the obstruction to a dam, constructed by Beaver. (Now that the bones and teeth of giant beavers, six to eight feet tall, are being uncovered, there may be more substance to the myth.) Mighty Glooscap thought the dam was a bad thing and cleaved it with his axe, with part of it floating out the harbour to make Partridge Island.

Dr. Barry Fell of Wales and, later, Harvard, an epigrapher, developed an interest in the Ogham script. This line and bar alphabet, originally without vowels, was in use by Celt-Iberians in Spain and Portugal and by ancient Irish from around 1300 to 100 BC. Examples of this writing have been found and deciphered by Dr. Fell in the New England states, Quebec, and Nova Scotia. An inscription on Manana Island, next to Monhegan, is said to translate into "Landing platform of the Phoenician traders". Another artifact has been found on McNutt's Island, near Shelburne, NS, and an upright rock, which looks like a pagan fertility symbol, is on the northeast promontory of Ghost Island in Belleisle Bay, off the St. John. A trip to Laconia, NH for aircraft modifications resulted in a visit to the "Stonehenge of America", where the sacrificial stone table was photographed, along with some of the stone works. There are channels on the margins of the altar to collect the blood, and there is a spout in the right lower edge to drain it.

Sacrificial stone, Nashua, NH

Stoneworks, Nashua, NH

White-robed Irish monks were reported to have been seen in North America before the arrival of the Northmen, but the Greenlanders Sagas' stories of Eric the Red and Lief the Lucky are authenticated by the discoveries of Helga Ingstad. The finding of butternuts, indigenous to the St. John River, in the Newfoundland settlement lends credence to a New Brunswick visit.

Prince Henry Sinclair was born in Scotland and had property there but he also inherited the Orkney Islands though Viking relationships. He was a seaman and built a strong navy that was to be reckoned with by other European principalities. In 1398, he mounted an expedition to the Atlantic coast of North America. A monument of a warrior bearing a shield with his coat of arms survives at Wexford Ledge, in Massachusetts. He is reported to have wintered at Cap d'Or, near Parrsboro at the head of the Bay of Fundy, and there is some question as to his responsibility for some of the Glooscap legends.

French fishermen from St. Malo were working the St. John in the 1500s and possibly earlier with their camp at Caton's Island. They were mostly Huguenots. In 1610, the Sieur de Biencourt, son of Poutrincourt, traveled from Port Royale to visit. The first Catholic church service on the St. John was held, converting the heathens, so that when subsequently executed, they died in the faith.

Charles LaTour roamed the woods of Acadia from 1608, trading out of the Port LaTour area of Nova Scotia and fighting with his father. He later set up business on the St. John, was declared Baronet of Nova Scotia by the British, and Governor of Acadia by the French. After his wife's death, following the defense of the fort in Saint John and Charles Menou's drowning from an overturned canoe, he married widow d'Aulnay. Thomas Temple became his partner on the river and took over after his death around 1655. Jurriaen Aernouts, a Dutch raider, was on the river in 1672, disturbing the Sieur de Soulanges and the few other French settlers.

Charles Le Moyne, Sieur d'Iberville, the "Cid of New French", appeared in St. John Harbour in 1696, aboard the *Envioux* and accompanied by the *Profond*. They confronted the English warships, *Sorlings* and *Newport*. The *Newport* was dismasted and surrendered. *Sorlings* escaped in the fog. D'Iberville proceeded to Pemaquid, just north of Boothbay to capture Fort William Henry and Captain Chubb. The fort was considered impregnable.

In reprisal, Major Ben Church was sent to demolish Villebon's new fort at the St. John. This was near where the Harbour Bridge toll booth now stands. When done, on his return trip to New England, he countered Colonel Hawthorne, who decided on an expedition up the river against Villebon at Fort Nashwaak. They were impeded by the Oromocto Shoals, so shallops were used for transport of men and cannon further upstream. A battery was set up on the south side of the Nashwaak River, opposite the fort but the siege was unsuccessful, the French losing one man, the English, eight.

Colonel Robert Monckton was sent to the St. John after the fall of Louisbourg in 1758 to secure Boishebert's fort, on the site of Villebon's at the mouth, which was in decay. It was rebuilt as Fort Frederick. The *Squirrel*, *Ulysses*, and *York* were sent up river, but the *Ulysses* struck what was probably Split Rock and sank immediately. The expedition was not pursued because it was October. A party of rangers was sent up during the winter on snowshoes under Captain McCurdy to destroy the French settlements. Captain McCurdy was killed when a man chopped down a tree, which fell on him, knocking him off a cliff at Kingston Creek. Lieutenant Moses Hazen finished the work, marching back on reversed snowshoes. He later became a general in the Continental Army, fighting for the Americans in the Lake Champlain campaigns.

After the arrival of the Loyalists, the St. John continued as the main highway for trade and commerce, using sail until after steamboat service became an option in 1816.

The activity of privateers during the War of 1812 is covered by C. H.J. Snider in his book *Under the Red Jack*. Caleb Seely was one of the more successful skippers under the letters of mark, captain of the *Star*, out of Saint John and later the *Liverpool Packet*. The latter was known, in after lives, as *Black Joke* and *Young Teazer's Ghost*. John Harris commanded the successful *Dart*. Others were the *General Smythe*, *Young William*, *Brunswicker*, and *Hunter*. *Hare* was sailed by James Reid, and *Sir John Sherbrooke*, by Thomas Robson, two vessels of the same name having been raiding from Halifax. John Coddington ran the *Comet* for Black & Company, and also, the *Herald*, for H. Johnson & Son and Thomas Millidge.

Mary, 1660, Royal Yacht of King Charles II, Internet source

Recreational sailing goes back to time immemorial. King Charles II acquired an affinity for sport sailing while exiled in Holland, where shallow draft, fast boast called yachts (derived from the German jager) were used to hunt… to imply a racing capability. On Charles II's return to Britain in 1660 for the Restoration the burgomaster of Amsterdam, Van Vlooswick, presented him with a vessel which he called the *Mary* after his sister, who was the widow of William II of Orange. This was the first royal yacht, and was used as such, for a year. Samuel Pepys, diarist and ship designer, and Peter Pett followed up with several more deeper drafted and without leeboards, for Charles' brother and illegitimate children. *Jamie* was named after the first child who later became Duke of Monmouth. *Folly* was Prince Rupert's and *Fan Fan*, the Duke of York's. The *Mary* was lost in the Irish Sea, during return from Dublin on anti-privateering duty.

The first group of vessels to be considered a yacht club was the Cork Water Club of 1720. The Royal Yacht Squadron was formed in 1815, with Lord Yarborough as commodore. He was noted for requiring his guests to sign consent for flogging prior to embarkation on his yacht, *Falcon*, which was also a naval auxiliary. Lord Yarborough introduced the port-starboard tack rule.

Sailing rules and conduct are based on the International Rules for the Prevention of Collision at Sea. These are expanded, elaborated and refined to govern yacht racing, which is considered a gentlemanly and non-contact sport. The discussion, on the water and at protest meetings, can ignite fiery verbal activity. Similar commotion can often be heard at handicap disagreements or between crew members on their own or competing craft.

Physical contact, such as the cutting of clew outhauls with a broad axe, intentional collision and other wanton destruction, is abhorred. A relatively recent incident which came before international rule bodies occurred at a European Finn class regatta in the 1960s, when an English competitor, a Mr. Pym, was annoyed by the proximity of his opponent, and cracked him over the knuckles with his paddle.

New Englanders became interested in the St. John River for trade in 1762. Mr. Blodgett was a financial backer from Boston and Mr. Hazen looked after business in Newburyport, while Simon and White ran the trading post in Saint John. They constructed a few schooners, the first of which was the *Betsy*. Real shipbuilding however began in the 1800s. Hundreds of sea-going vessels were built between 1800 and 1900 at just about any site where lumber was available, including unlikely places such as Norton and Welsford, from where unballasted craft must have come with the freshet, before bridges were built in these areas. Some of the fastest ships in the world came out of Saint John yards. Ten ships recorded runs of over four hundred nautical miles in twenty-four hours, and two were from Saint John; the others were from the United States. *Champion of the Seas*, a MacKay clipper from Boston constructed for the Black Ball Line, claimed an uncertified four hundred and sixty-nine mile passage. *Lightning*, a MacKay clipper for the Black Ball sailed by Captain Enright had four hundred and thirty-six and four hundred and thirty mile runs on her maiden voyage from Boston to Liverpool. *Marco Polo* is credited with four hundred and twenty-eight miles under Captain MacDonald. Nevin's *Shalimar* is credited with four hundred and twenty. With the slowing of commercial sailing after 1890, many of the families involved continued sailing for recreation.

Robert Thomson was in charge of the William Thomson Steamship Company, and had a major interest in yachting, having had the ninety-two-foot steam yacht *Scionda* built in New York. Thomson served as commodore of the Royal Kennebecasis Yacht Club from 1901 to 1912.

J. Fraser Gregory, of the lumber company, owned the motor yacht, *Zuleika*, fifty-four feet ten inches. He had the logs of several yacht club cruises and autumn duck hunts printed, excerpts of which have been included, courtesy of Thomas Chesworth of the Williams family.

Three big "H" names in Saint John yachting were Holders, sailmakers from the 1860s to the present, now under Mac Ester; the Heans, builders; and the Herringtons, also builders. The Applebys ran a ship yard at East Riverside and are still active sailors.

Captain Sullivan was in the British army and his son Dennis was in Nelson's navy. Old Thomas Hilyard came from Devon and captained a ship for the Barlows of Saint John. He married Margaret Miles, daughter of Thomas Miles, silversmith from New York living at York Point. Young Thomas was born in 1810 and his mother became a widow in 1816. She married Dennis Sullivan in 1818, and had five more children. Young Thomas did well in the lumber business and had a sawmill at the end of a causeway that ran to Hilyard's Reef, where the eastern pillars of the harbour bridge are imbedded. He purchased the old Haws' yard, extending his property, and began ship building in 1852 through a connection with the Ruddocks, in the midst of the Australian gold rush. His younger half-brother, Joseph Sullivan, became master builder and yard foreman. Thirty-nine ships were constructed between 1852 and 1877 when the yard closed. Joseph then moved the family to Kouchibouguac, where he built for MacLeod, including the *Dunstainage*. He returned to Saint John in 1884 to work for the Sayres, who launched seven vessels. The last was the *Vamoose*, in 1891, the year he died.

Joseph Sullivan

Vamoose

| Builder: | Frederick E. Sayre | Tonnage: | 348.73 tons |
| Launched: | Saint John, New Brunswick 1891 | Artist: | Anonymous |

Vamoose, *courtesy of New Brunswick Museum*

Canada, *1998*

Yachts at Millidgeville,
Saint John, New Brunswick, c.1894

Yachts, Thetis, Canada *and* Sunol, *c. 1990*

Royal Kennebecasis Yacht Club Vessels, including the Yacht, Primrose,
at Fredericton, New Brunswick, 1895. Courtesy of the New Brunswick Museum

RKYC 1904

SQUADRON LIST.

SAILING YACHTS.

CLASS A.— ALL OVER 30 FEET RACING LENGTH.

Club Signal Letters.	Numbers. Racing. Registered	Name.	Rig.	K. or C.B.	Length Over All Act.	Length Over All Reg.	LWL	R.L.	Depth.	Register'd Net Ton.	Sail Area.	Owner.	Designer.	Builder.	Port of Registry.
W. M. N.	19 / 107078	Ariel,	Cutter,	C.B.	30.	37.0	29.0	31.6	4.4	6.83	1140	Robert Mathew.	J. T. Logan.	J. T. Logan.	St. John.
W. N. B.	23	Armorel,	Cutter,	C.B.	36.6	......	24.8	30.5			1316	Lindsay Parker.	H. J. Gielow.	J. T. Logan.	St. John.
W. H. J.	1 / 107531	Canada,	Sloop,	C.B.	42.0	36.2	31.3	36.5	.0	8.45	1753	Fred S. Heans. Howard Holder. Howard Camp.	Robt. McIntyre.	Wm. Heans, Sr.	St. John.
W. S. T.	42	Mavis,	Cutter,	K.	61.0	......	43.0	52.0	.0	29.	3700	Travis Cochran.	E. Ross.	E. Ross.	Philadelphia, U.S.
W. P. B.	31 / 107792	Windward,	Schr.,	C.B.	56.0	49.2	47.4	43.4	5.2	24.17	2546	R. S. Ritchie. T. U. Hay. W. White et al.	E. Burgess.	E. Burgess.	St. John.
W. B. H.	22 / 112221	Dahinda,	Schr.,	K.	......	54.4			6.7	36.14		W. M. McKay.	A. N. Harned.	A. N. Harned.	St. John.
W. J. B.	14 / 112227	Louvima,	Cutter,	K.	45.0	40.3	34.9	38.2	7.0	15.33	1825	H. R. Dunn. J. H. Kimball. F. J. Likely. A. H. Likely.	A. N. Harned.	A. N. Harned.	St. John.
W. B. J.	18 / 111880	Columbia,	Schr.,	K.	61.	......	39.9		8.0	22.		Frank Lovitt.	G. Lawley & Son.	G. Lawley & Son.	Yarmouth N.S.
W. B. M.	13	Hermes II.,	Sloop,	K.	57.6		40.		8.6		2500	I. A. Lovitt.	Rice Bros.	Rice Bros.	"

138   139

SAILING YACHTS — CONTINUED.

CLASS B.— NOT OVER 30 FEET AND OVER 25 FEET RACING LENGTH.

Club Signal Letters.	Numbers. Racing. Registered	Name.	Rig.	K. or C.B.	Length Over All Act.	Length Over All Reg.	LWL	R.L.	Depth.	Register'd Net Ton.	Sail Area.	Owner.	Designer.	Builder.	Port of Registry.
W. L. M.	27 / 111504	Avis,	Sloop,	K.	......	31.	25.1	27.5	2.9	4.25		W. R. Turnbull,	......	......	St. John.
W. M. H.	24 / 107079	British Queen,	Sloop,	C.B.	30.	27.	25.1	27.5	2.8	4.29	800	Chas. Kain.	E. Ross.	E. Ross.	St. John.
W. J. H.	7	Gracie M.,	Sloop,	K.	31.7	28.6	24.1	27.8	3.4	6.46	994	Chas. E. Elwell.	M. McLean.	Geo. Washburn.	St. John.
W. M. P.	20	Irex,	Sloop,	C.B.	36.3	......	22.0	25.8	1.0	3.34	882	R. M. Fowler.	E. Burgess.	J. T. Logan.	St. John.
W. H. P.	4 / 107532	Jubilee,	Sloop,	K.	31.5	25.2	25.5	28.	3.1	4.84	932	H. Alison	J. Logan.	J. T. Logan.	St. John.
W. M. T.	15 / 107538	Mowgli,	Sloop,	K.	29.3	24.4	22.5	25.4	3.8	4.51	809	F. H. J. Ruel.	W. E. Waterhouse.	W. H. Butler.	St. John
W. M. N.	26 / 107799	Bert,	Sloop,	K.	31.1	25.2	25.8	26.2	3.1	4.24	791	T. W. McNichol.	J. C. McCluskey.	J. C. McCluskey.	St. John.
W. J. N.	10 / 107536	Rose,	Sloop,	K.	32.3	25.	23.6	26.8	3.0	4.91	862	A. H. Merrill et al	E. McGuiggan.	E. McGuiggan.	St. John
W. J. M.	9 / 107076	Sunol,	Sloop,	K.	31.	27.	25.4	29.5	3.9	5.92	1146	W. Stratton et al.	C. McL. Troop.	D. Lynch.	St. John
W. B. N.	11	Edna,	....	K.	30.	......			4.6			H. Ellis.	H. Ellis.	E. Ross.	St. John.
W. M. P.	29 / 107541	Taniwha,	Sloop,	K.	36.9	33.3	27.0	27.4	4.2	6.04	782	W. A. Maclauchlan	J. N. Sutherland.	A. N. Harned.	St. John.

140   RKYC   1904   141

SAILING YACHTS — CONTINUED.

CLASS B. — NOT OVER 30 FEET AND OVER 25 FEET RACING LENGTH.

Club Signal Letters.	Numbers. Racing. Registered	Name.	Rig.	K. or C.B.	Length Over All. Act.	Length Over All. Reg.	L.W.L.	R.L.	Beam.	Depth.	Registered Net Ton.	Sail Area.	Owner.	Designer.	Builder.	Port of Registry.
W. M. H.	17 / —	Venus.	Sloop,	K.	28.		25.1	27.0	10.5	4.	7.99	...	K. Pedersen.	J. T. Logan.	J. T. Logan.	St. John.
W. H. M.	2 / 107800	Wahbewawa.	Sloop,	C. B.	37.7	32.2	26.3	29.2	15.1	4.1	8.25	1030	H. Gilbert, Jr.	H. Gilbert, Jr.	J. T. Logan.	St. John.
W. H. T.	5 / 107539	Winogene.	Cutter.	C. B.	36.	29.0	25.9	28.5	10.5	3.2	6.85	974	M. J. Trueman.	W. Brittain.	W. Brittain.	St. John.
W. B. P.	28 / 107345	Hermes.	Sloop,	C. B.	36.6				11.		4.08		I. A. Lovett.			Yarmouth N. S.
W. B. S.	33	Petrel.	Sloop,	K.	32.		26.	25.	8.	4.6	4.50	650	H. Holder.	D. Munro.	D. Munro.	St. John.

CLASS C — NOT OVER 25 FEET AND OVER 20 FEET RACING LENGTH.

Club Signal Letters.	Numbers. Racing. Registered	Name.	Rig.	K. or C.B.	Length Over All. Act.	Length Over All. Reg.	L.W.L.	R.L.	Beam.	Depth.	Registered Net Ton.	Sail Area.	Owner.	Designer.	Builder.	Port of Registry.
W. H. S.	6 / 107073	Bluenose.	Sloop,	K	27.	23.2	22.6	22.3	8.	2.3	2.40	490	Geo. E. Holder.	D. McLauchlin.	D. McLauchlin.	St. John.
W. J. S.	12 / 107075	Edna.	Sloop,	K	28.	24.8	20.1	23.0	7.3	2.3	2.81	476	W. H. McIntyre.	R. Crealock.	R. Crealock.	St. John.
W. S. M.	46	Ethel M.	Sloop,	K	27.0		18.6	30.6	9.9			510	Wm. McAvity.	W. McAvity.	W. J. McShane.	St. John.
W. T. H.	44	Hesperus.	Sloop,	C B	27.		24.	23.0	8.	3.0		450	A. C. Fairweather.	P. Griffiths.	P. Griffiths.	St. John.
W. H. M.	3 / 107543	Kathleen.	Sloop,	C B	26.6	23.2	22.8	24.8	9.	3.6	3.50	731	A. McArthur et al.	E. Burgess.	J. T. Logan.	St. John.

142   143

SAILING YACHTS — CONTINUED.

CLASS C. — NOT OVER 25 FEET AND OVER 20 FEET RACING LENGTH.

Club Signal Letters.	Numbers. Racing. Registered	Name.	Rig.	K. or C.B.	Length Over All. Act.	Length Over All. Reg.	L.W.L.	R.L.	Beam.	Depth.	Registered Net Ton.	Sail Area.	Owner.	Designer.	Builder.	Port of Registry.
W. H. R.	8	Kelpie.	Sloop,	K	28.	24.4	23.	24.7	10.	2.3	1.83	496	H. Azbe.	G. L. Watson.	R. D. Butler.	St. John.
W. S. B.	14	Lakeside.	Sloop,	C B	22.		20.6	21.0	6.8			480	Jas. A. McAvity.	James Odell.	Jas. Odell.	St. John.
W. S. H.	38 / 107801	Myrtle.	Sloop,	K	30.	25.5	23.0	24.4	8.4	3.0	1.52	641	F. Herrington.	John George.	John George.	St. John.
W. B. T.	17	Whitecap.	Schr.	C B	24.8				7.5				B. D. Paterson.	Wm. Stewart.	Wm. Stewart.	St. John.
W. M. J.	25 / 107544	Robin Hood.	Sloop,	K	29.6	23.7	21.4	24.7	9.	3.2	1.54	780	T. T. Lantalum.	H. F. Widdleton.	W. H. Butler.	St. John.
W. N. S.	30	Skookum.	Sloop,	K	25.3		21.2	21.2	7.5	3.6		730	Geo. Francis Kerr.	F. H. Myles.	F. H. Myles.	St. John.
W. S. J.	30	Undine.	Cat.	C B	24.0		18.6	20.0	9.	2.0		430	Robt. Mathews.		Jas. T. Logan.	St. John.
W. J. P.	49	Aianna.	Sloop,	C B	27.6		20.		10.4	1.7			Lindsay Parker.	H. J. Gielow.	A. N. Harned.	St. John.
W. J. T.	21	Glencairn IV.	Sloop,	C B	36.2		25.	25.0	8.	0.3	1.10	740	W. B. Ganong.	G. H. Duggan.	J. C. McCluskey.	St. John.
W. M. J.	31	Privateer.	Sloop,	K	30.7		22.6		9.2				J. C. McCluskey.	J. C. McCluskey.	J. C. McCluskey.	St. John.

144

R K Y C
SAILING YACHT

CLASS D. — NOT OVER TWENT[...]

Club Signal Letters.	Numbers. Racing. Registered	Name.	Rig.	K. or C. B.	Length Over All. Act.	Length Over All. Reg.	LWL	R. L.	Beam
W. P. T.	37	Asthore,	Sloop,	C B	17.	....	14.0	13.9	
W. P. H.	32	Clytie,	Sloop,	C B	25.	....	19.8	19.9	
W. M. B.	16	Marguerite,	Sloop,	C B	20.4	....	18.6	16.9	
W. M T.	35	Phantom,	Sloop,	C B	29	....	16 0	17.6	
....		Atalanta,	Sloop,	C B	26.8	....	....		

CLASS E.

T. W. P.	....	Kenwood.	2-Sail.	C B	23.	....	21.6	....	
T. W. B.	....	Elite.	"	C B	21 0	....	21.0	....	
T. W. H.	....	Nemo.	"	C B	21.6	....	21 6	....	
T. W. N.	....	Umtata.	"	C B	22.0	....	22.0	....	
W. P. M	....	Defender.	"	C B	27.0	....	22.0	....	
....		Anona,	"	C B	26.0	....	23.	....	
....		Atlantic,	"	C B	26.8	....	23	....	

146

1904   145

CONTINUED.

ET RACING LENGTH.

Register'd Net Ton.	Sale Area.	Owner.	Designer.	Builder.	Port of Registry.
....	185	W. B. Ganong	Robt. Davidson	Robt. Davidson	St. John
....	406	P. Egan	H. Gilbert, jr.	H. Gilbert, jr.	St. Johd
....	225	W. B. Ganong	W. Logan	W. Logan	St. John
....	374	A. J. Machum	C. A. Machum	C. A. Machum	St. John
....	190	Noel F. Sheraton	Ed. Hampton	Ed. Hampton	St. John

IFF CLASS.

....	355	W. W. Allen	E. Ross	E. Ross	St. John
....	240	Geo. Waring			St. John
....	250	F. P. Starr			St. John
....	290	Geo. L. Warwick	John George	John George	St. John
....	350	Horace King	A. H. Harned	A. H. Harned	St John
....	325	John Frodsham	C. W. Shamper	C. W. Shamper	St. John
....	360	Louis Munro et al	— Anderson	— Anderson	St. John

Log of the Yacht "Zuleika"

Leaving Millidgeville 11th July, 1908, on
the twelfth Annual Cruise of
The Royal Kennebecasis Yacht Club.

The crew properly "signed on" in their various capacities was

J. Fraser Gregory	Captain & Owner
Mrs. F. E. Williams	Mate
J. James McCaskill	Flag Officer
F. E. Williams	Chief Engineer
N. A. Earp	Able-bodied Seaman
Mrs. Alice Winters	Super-cargo
Miss Ora Rutherford	Secretary
Mrs. J. F. Gregory	Hostess

Behold the handsome group:

At six bells in the afternoon the Commodore fired the starting gun from the Flag-ship "Scionda" and the signal P. I. N. (Belleisle) went to the masthead. At once the yachts commenced filling out the eastern channel from the Club anchorage. More than half a gale was blowing from the southwest. All the sailors were close reefed and we could see from the way they careened that there would be heavy weather in the Bay and Long Reach.

At seven bells the Flag-ship started and we followed almost immediately. As the gale was fair the sailors had no difficulty in keeping up with the power boats and sometimes passed them. In Grand Bay the "Louvima" passed us.

At Brandy Point we spied the "Edna", which had preceded us, ashore on the bar, but as the Flag-ship was on her way to the rescue we did not stop to assist. Capt. Rodgerson of the "Edna", and veteran of the Fleet, being seventy-four years of age, told us later that in his difficulties in managing his small Boat in the gale he forgot all about his course with the result narrated.

At Westfield we dropped anchor for a few minutes just above the wharf and saw the finish of an exciting salmon boat race. While at anchor the Fleet closed up rapidly, several of the Yachts passing us Tuesday, 14th.

The sun rose bright in a clear sky without a breath of wind indicating another hot day. Our Captain was astir earlier than usual as he wished to make some pictures and visit the Saw Mills of F. E. Sayre & Company.

As the Fleet lay in the River it was impossible to get a picture of the Fleet as a whole but we have a very good picture of the Bridge, "Scionda", "Zulekia" and "Louvima".

the crews of the "Vagabond" and "Louvima" in undress uniform hob-nobbing aboard the first named Yacht.

At 10.15 the tows started down River in the same order as they had come up the previous day but at a smarter pace, the result of our Captain's urging the Commodore to go faster and keep out of his way.

But we must not forget to tell you that at Chipman our flag-officer actually and literally stole a supply of ice from the ice-house on the wharf.

The wind rose as we ran down the River and the word was passed along that the Yachts would race from Cox's Point to Robertson's Point.

Other Sullivan ancestors include James Segee, captain of the *General Smythe*, the first steamboat on the river and the Stevens, who descended from Shubael, a Loyalist from Connecticut, who settled at Brandy Point. Stephen Stevens was a surveyor of timber, while Robert and John were tugboat men. Robert was captain of the *Transit*, which was running at night in the spring of 1852 when it collided with the riverboat, *Anna Augusta*, whose boiler exploded, scalding four people to death by steam. No fault was found, but the need for improved navigation rules was advised. Captain John Stevens was said to be the first to tow a raft of logs through the Reversing Falls by tug. In 1856, old Captain John was a member of the Indiantown crew for a rowing race against Carleton. He wagered his house on the race, although the West Siders were heavy favourites. The course was out the harbour, around Partridge Island, and back. On the way in from the island, with Carleton in the lead, the Indiantowners, spotting a defect in one of the large weirs on the west side, rowed through, taking the lead and holding it to the finish. It was claimed that "They took the rag from Carleton's brag."

The Early Yachtsmen

By spring of 1894, the idea of a yacht club ripened, and in May, Frank Whelpley, Albert McArthur, Howard Holder and Fred Heans met in the *Dolphin* or *Naiad* to form the Saint John Yacht Club. The anchorage was at Indiantown, but many preferred Millidgeville. A vote was held and the move approved. A decision was also made to name the new club after the river on which it was situated in 1898. Some people still preferred Indiantown, which one could reach by streetcar, formed the Saint John Boat Club, and stayed in Marble Cove. The object of the club was to promote motor boats, sailing, rowing, and canoeing, and to encourage its members in becoming proficient in navigation, the personal management, control and handling of their boats, to establish and enforce uniform rules for the government of races and to provide the necessary club accommodation. This became the Saint John Powerboat Club.

The Corporation Cup was presented for racing in 1894, and an event was staged for the first time on August 21 of that year. The yachts *Sunol*, Patrick Egan; *Maple Leaf*, Elijah Ross; *Primrose*, Samuel Hutton; and *Gracie M.*, Charles Elwell, competed. The yachts were sitting off the west end of Mahogany Island when a severe northwest line squall hit, damaging all boats. The *Primrose* filled and sank immediately. Eight of her twelve man crew drowned, including her skipper, a member of the Paris (rowing) Crew. Howard Holder saved himself by holding onto an upturned bucket. It was believed that if cannon were fired, bodies would rise to the surface but only one was recovered. The craft was later raised and sailed again. The tragedy struck home, and it was 1934 before another race in the harbour was sponsored.

Joseph Sullivan's only surviving son, Herman, worked for Gilbert, Bent & Son and later joined T. H. Estabrook as his accountant and first employee. A charter member of the Saint John Boat Club, and its long time treasurer, he won a little motor boat, the *Bunny*, in a raffle. This was easier than rowing up to Acamac on Saturday night after the shops closed. These were open boats with a tarp and drapes on the sides, suspended by four posts, to keep out some of the weather. The *Bunny* was replaced by the *LaTour* which was a bit bigger. On a spring weekend in the early 1900s, Sullivan's boys became eager to launch. This was done in a rush, without the usual caulking and painting. A fine cruise was had to Belyea's Point, followed by pitching a tent on shore and anchoring the boat off. They slept well until early morning, when awakened by Grenville Ring's booming voice, roaring from the fog, "Hey! Sullivan! Your eelpot sunk."

The *Canada* was designed by Robert McIntyre of Boston and built by William Heans, at the end of Main Street, by Likely's mill pond, for Fred Heans, Howard Holder, and Howard Camp. She was a gaff-rigged sloop, with topsail, and forty-two feet in length. She was launched in 1898, with little Harry Heans aboard. She was fast, locally, and competed with *Cibou* of Sydney, Nova Scotia, for the Coronation Cup, presented by Robert Thomson in 1902. The cup went to Nova Scotia, and a challenge was made in 1903 by RKYC with the *Glencairn IV*, a scow type of craft of W. B. Ganong, brought from Montreal. This race was held in Cape Breton and *Cibou* won again. The cup has been in Nova Scotia ever since. The *Canada* had a centerboard, had a Phoenix make-and-break engine installed as she matured, and had her rig changed to a yawl. She was moored for years above Harding's Point, a familiar sight while waiting for the ferry. Major Bill Gamblin, who made molded plywood planing dinghies, and had family up at the Narrows on the Washadomoak, took the vessel to Ottawa to upgrade it.

Restoration has been slow but another group restarted the program a few years ago. The *Canada* is still the only vessel of the name on the Canadian Registry. In the winter, the *Canada*'s rig was transferred to an ice boat, and old stern steerer, which would hold up to thirteen people. It was said to sound like a freight train going up and down the Kennebecasis.

The Canada

In 1904, Saint John celebrated the tercentenary of the St. Croix landing by the French. There were still many shipwrights around, permitting the RKYC to contribute to the pageant. A St. John River woodboat was converted into a replica of Champlain's ship, which sailed the harbour, surrounded by RKYC members clad in native dress and paddling canoes. One of the "warriors" was Ned Herrington, captain of the *O Yes*, yacht builder and sailor. A painting of the event is preserved by the RKYC.

The *Vagabond* was another survivor. She was on the yacht club cruise of 1908 and was owned by Walter Logan. Guy Lordly, chief chemist at the sugar refinery, had her for years and moored her in Drury Cove, where she was a fixture and quite picturesque. Rev. George Akerley bought her around 1969 and put the sails to her for the first time in years, a wonder to see. She was in collision with the *Whistler*, a Northwind 29, at the start of a race in 1970, and suffered some damage to the bowsprit and stem. St. Andrews interests acquired her next and Reg Brown Jr. sailed down the Bay. She returned to Millidgeville and Colonel Holder's yard. Her back was broken and she burned in a disastrous fire in 1982.

The *Rena M.* was a pretty schooner with a clipper bow, owned by Fred Mullin in the 1920s and 30s. She was about fifty-two feet, had three jibs, topsails and a fisherman. She was sold to Dr. E. A. Petrie, head of radiology at St. Joseph's Hospital in the 1940s, and he had her rebuilt at Richardson's on Deer Island in 1957, with a Bermuda main. Dr. Petrie liked hot Colman's mustard in his sandwiches and disliked a cleated mainsheet, which was a cause of many a capsize before the quick release.

The *Wanderer* was owned by Howie Holder in the 1920s as a gaff rigger but had a jib-headed main in the 1950s when Tom Chesworth Sr. sailed her.

Yacht, Windward, *c. 1910, Courtesy of New Brunswick Museum*
Length 56 feet, Owners R.S. Ritchie, T.U. Hay, W. White

The Villian, *1926*
Courtesy of New Brunswick Museum

Yacht, Winogene, *16 August 1914*
M.J. Trueman, 36 feet
Courtesy of New Brunswick Museum

Yacht, Wanderer, *12 October 1924, Owner, Howie Holder*
Courtesy of New Brunswick Museum

The *Syce* was brought to Saint John after being constructed for the world six metre championships. She failed to qualify. She was very close winded, and Ned Herrington, who sailed her, was asked how she did on the Long Reach in a southwester. He said "in one hitch." When asked about weathering Craig's Point, he replied, "Give her a little luff." The *Syce* was mahogany and had a finish like a grand piano. Bernie Ralston sailed her in the 1940s and she was just about unbeatable. Bernie played basketball for the *Saint Johns* and refereed rugby games among other things. He moved to New York to become athletic director in the New York Police Department. *Syce* was sold to Bob Damery and went to Nova Scotia in 1949. A photograph from 1948, courtesy of Bev Appleby, shows the *Syce*, moored at Gondola Point after a race, with crew. On the beach, behind Bernie's head, can be seen the last riverboat, *D. J. Purdy*. She discontinued service in 1947, was beached to be a dance hall in the spring, and burned soon after.

In the 1920s, Major Gordon Holder, later Colonel, went shopping for a yacht, driving down to Nova Scotia. At the Royal Nova Scotia Yacht Squadron, he and his companion saw a nice looking boat but continued the tour down to Lunenburg to see what else was available. They saw some fine craft, however no decision was made. On the way back, they stopped in at the Squadron again and the original boat looked like the best candidate. By that time, they had had a couple of drinks of rum and an attitude adjustment, so the vessel was named the *Merry Major*. She was later owned by Dr. "Dutch" Kee, Ralph Munro, Cleve Belyea, and Garnet Phinney. She had many modifications to the cabin top and internal layout, was coated with fibreglass and sailed into the 1990s. Cleve had particularly good success racing her.

The *Nemac*, also named *Melita* and *Keora*, was around in the 1920s, a gaff-rigged yawl. F. Patterson Coombs owned her, and later, Reg Brown Sr. of the Brown Box Company. Reg Brown Jr. was raised on this vessel and on the *Princess*, a sixty-foot, "hump backed" schooner. He sailed *Nemac* in the Digby Race of 1952, when Mr. A. C. Glennie was thrown into the water from his yacht, *Marina* near Digby. He was recovered but died a few minutes later from a heart attack. The return trip to Saint John on Sunday featured a gale with gusts to sixty knots, with the *Canada* fetching St. Martins and the *Savitar* of Colonel Holder fetching Musquash. The *Atlanta* had major damage to her sails. The *Nemac* was sold to Roly Black and became *Keora* again, receiving aluminum spars and a Bermuda rig. She was cruised extensively and sold to Derek Hamilton, who did more restoration. "Rock" Belyea has been working on her lately and still has her sailing.

In 1932, Ruth Nichols was attempting to become the first woman to fly solo across the Atlantic. Her Lockheed Vega landed at the Saint John Airport in Millidgeville but crashed on takeoff into the trees near Bedell Avenue. She suffered fractures and became one of the first patients at the new Saint John General Hospital. Geoff and John Sayre sailed down from Rothesay in the *Junco* to see the crash site. Ms. Nichols' manager arrived with another Vega and Geoff had his first flight sitting on an orange crate. He flew in Coastal Command during the war and has been a great iceboat enthusiast.

SYCE
Courtesy of Harrison Studios

Six metre class

Snipes

A group of yachtsmen met at Rothesay and decided to organize a local yacht club in 1909. Many of the boats were also members of RKYC or SJPBC.

The *Soangetaha*, twenty-six feet, was a broad-beamed, centerboard, skimming dish with a self-tacking jib and no cabin. She was built in the 1920s and owned by the Tennants and Fred Toole. She was always well kept and later sailed by Oakley Gould and finally, Bill Hurley in the late 1930s. She was wrecked in a northerly gale in the autumn of 1940 on the rocks at Acamac. Bill was called up to the army.

The *Sunol* was long lasting, having sailed in the Corporation Cup Race of 1894. H. E. Sullivan liked to tell of a trip down the Washademoak, blown overboard to leeward and flipping like a rag doll on the end of the jib sheet. She was owned by Mr. W. Stratton and moored in Courtney Bay at times in the winter. Stratton became blind and used to walk Princess and Orange Streets with his Collie. The thirty-one foot vessel sank in Drury Cove in the 1930s.

Herman E. and Charlie C. Sullivan turned in the *LaTour* in 1914 for the *Senator*, which had a proper cabin with a *Little Cod* for duck hunting until freeze up. They switched to the *Foam*, in the 1920s, which had been a test bed for Fairbanks-Morse. The cabin format was altered and she was quite comfortable. The Allens bought her in 1937. The tender was about eleven feet, lap straked and round bottomed. There was a hole drilled in the bow seat to step a mast with a sprit sail. It was fine on a reach or downwind but, having no board, had to be rowed to windward.

Dave Pirie owned a grocery store on Coburg Street, across from the head of Peters Street. He spent a lot of time carving soap sculptures, which were very good. He was also a member of the *Maritime Merchants Association*, or MMA, which had an office on Union Street. As well, he belonged to the Royal Kennebecasis Yacht Club, where his eighteen foot, lap straked, centerboard, sliding Gunter rigged sloop was moored. On fine summer afternoons, Dave would inform his staff that he was off to the MMA or "Emma May," whatever she was named.

In 1937, the Sullivans bought her and headed out for the old Stevens farm at Acamac. It was about two miles, but with no wind, the trip took six hours, and supper was cold. Life vests were worn and she filled a few times in Grand Bay, but always made it home. She sat upside down through the winter so no one could drop a screwdriver between the planks in the spring. She became another victim of a fall norther in 1941, on the rocks at Acamac.

Ned Herrington's sons, Bayard and Cecil (Pat) were fast dinghy racers of the 1920s and 1930s, in fourteen-foot internationals. Bayard raced *Tut-Tut* and was always looking for a challenge at the Venetian Nights, held in Indiantown by the Power Boat Club after the war. He skippered a couple of races in a jollyboat in the 1960s. He worked for G. E. Barbour and threatened to put wheels on the *O Yes* when they moved him to Sussex. Pat donated countless hours to race committee work but a bad heart deterred him from getting on a boat. After many years, he decided to try it and had a cardiac arrest on the starting line in the cockpit of Nevin Burnham's schooner, *Mary J*. Attempts at resuscitation were unsuccessful.

Soangetaha

unknown

Gordie Wark on the helm

Soangetaha

Senator

Dot Wark

MOTOR YACHTS 1938

HAPPY DAYS	R. K. & R. S. MILLER
JENICHA	REG. & C. WINTER-BROWN
JOAN	G. KING KELLY
MADE OF THE MISSED	HUGH MacKAY
PENGUIN ISLAND	L. H. DYER
SEA PRINCE	ARTHUR HAZEN
x SNOVER	R. D. PATERSON
SALLY	THOS. R. STEEVES
SAXON	JAS. PLOMER
x SWAN	Dr. A. E. MACAULAY
TRITON	F. D. MacLENNAN
x TANTRAMAR	SENATOR F. B. BLACK
WEKENDA	E. N. HERRINGTON

x- Admiralty Warrant   —   o- Canadian Warrant

LISTS AS OF MAY 1st.

YACHT	TIME ALLOWANCE	10 MILES
ADERYN	22 MINUTES	
AESCA	13 MINUTES	
CANADA	12 MINUTES	
DAHINDA	1 MINUTES	
FIE YUEN	15 MINUTES	
FALCON	15 MINUTES	
GULL	— MINUTES	
GRACIE M	18 MINUTES	
MERRY MAJOR	6 MINUTES	
MARINA 1	14 MINUTES	
NOR-WESTER	— MINUTES	
NAIAD	32 MINUTES	
NEMAC	20 MINUTES	
OLD GLORY	20 MINUTES	
OSPREY	14 MINUTES	
PAKWAN	14 MINUTES	
PRINCESS	8 MINUTES	
PATCHES	22 MINUTES	
PELICAN	15 MINUTES	
RENA M.	15 MINUTES	
SURF	22 MINUTES	
SPRAY	19 MINUTES	
SPINDRIFT	22 MINUTES	
SYCE (Scratch)	— MINUTES	
SMOKE	5 MINUTES	
SAVETAR	18 MINUTES	
VILLIAN	32 MINUTES	
VAGABOND	6 MINUTES	
WANDERER	17 MINUTES	
WU YUEN	18 MINUTES	
WHISTLER	12 MINUTES	
ZETES	6 MINUTES	

LIST AS OF MAY 1ST
(S SUBJECT TO CHANGE)

SMALL BOATS of R. K. Y. C.

BOAT	NO.	OWNER
ALL RITE	40	TOM WRIGHT
MITZIE	29	BILL WETMORE
MIST	31	KEN ELWELL
NIKI	41	MALCOLM NICKERSON
O'WASKA	42	LLOYD WHITEBONE
RIPPLE	35	LARRY MOFFORD
SCOUT	47	BERNIE MITCHELL
SUNRAY	46	ARTHUR COLLINS
SCAMPER	45	DON HARTT
VENTURE	34	DON HOLDER
VIKING	30	G. G. K. HOLDER, Jr.
WINGS	48	GORDON SMITH

Sailing at Grand Bay

Sailing at Belyea's Point

The Rothesay Yacht Club presented the MacKay Trophy in 1930, for interclub team racing with RKYC, with four of the fastest boats from each club competing. Mac Grant had owned the Tancook Schooner, *Pelican*, but moved to a Chester C class yacht from Nova Scotia in the 1930s, the *Gannet*. Her first landfall on the sail to New Brunswick was Gannet Rock, hence her name. She has won a lot of races over the years and is a Grant family heirloom.

In the 1930s, design classes were becoming popular, with the idea of giving level racing between crews. The Star class was an early example and some were built in the area. The *Spray* and the *Surf* were similar fine-lined keelboats, which were fast and modern. The Snipe class, designed by William F. Crosby, and relatively easy to build in garage or basement, proliferated more rapidly. The class spread over North and South America and is still raced widely. They were sailed around Saint John before, during, and after the war. There was a fleet at the RKYC, some of them constructed at the *Blue Peter* boat works of Don Holder. Crosby also designed the Seagull class, two examples of which were Norm Herrington's *Banshee* and Eldon Card's *Cossack*. The Snipe was fifteen feet without a spinnaker, while the Seagull looked similar but was larger, about eighteen feet. Another Crosby design was the National One Design, which looked like a Snipe forward but had an inboard rudder, which made it hard to beach, and overhanging stern and a tall aspect rig. By its appearance, it should have been fast and outperformed the Snipe, but never did, and this was verified at several *Yachting* magazine one-design regattas. Audrey (Turner) Sweeney was hard to beat in her Snipe, *Briney Marlin*, and she used the name for her first cruising boat. In her youth, before there was Kennebecasis Drive, Audrey used to row down from the Turner farm and back to do her sailing. Her current boat, a Nordin Ballad 30, whose prototype won the European Half Ton Championship, *Malabeam*, is named after the Maliseet princess who led the Mohawk raiders to their destruction over Grand Falls. Audrey was usually the small-boat winner at the Renforth Regatta, which was renewed after the war, with yacht races in all classes and canoeing and swimming competitions. Canoe tilting was a lark.

The yacht, *Sphinx*, was a member of the Royal Yacht Squadron in the 1860s in the era of and rating for, the American's Cup Races. She was one of the first yachts to fly a balloon jib, which was called "Sphinx's Acre," shortened, later, to spinnaker.

In 1947, the sail-off for the Royals Regatta was won by Reg Brown Jr. with crew of Joe Streeter and Lloyd Pratt in RKYC club Snipes. The Royals are held sporadically, usually to celebrate an event like an anniversary. They are held at a Royal yacht club, with a crew from each other Royal yacht club invited as competitors. This regatta was in Halifax, in Bluenoses designed by Roue. Reg had good boat speed but the vagaries of the wind in Halifax Harbour and some of the course changes by the race committee mystified him.

The *Djinn* was the fastest of the Micmac 22 Foot class, a Maritime development. It had a twenty-two foot keelboat, sloop-rigged with few other restrictions. The *Djinn*, a product of Don Holder and Dr. Bernie Skinner, had a fairly beamy, almost scow-like hull and won her share of races the first year and after. She had a double cockpit, which Bev Appleby opened up when he acquired her, and changed the name to *Ricklyn*. Dr. Skinner also had a swift-looking, low freeboard racer about that time, the *Cossack*, which he and Bayard Herrington took to Montreal. Other vessels of the Micmac class were the *Mic*, the *Mac*, Pat Staples; the *Micmac*, Fred Page; the *Migsie*, Elwood Johnston, later Lyle Dyer; the *Jeep*, the *Moby Dick*, Bob Barton, later Dr. I. Karrell; the *Banreigh*, Mac Somerville, Charlie Kee, Dr. Barry Beckett.

Don, *National One Design*

Avalanche. *Built by Russel McNamara*
Owned by Dr. S. Weyman and Bill Fearnhead

Sigma. *Robert Quinlan, Pat McBride, Mrs. Quinlan, Bootsie Quinlan, Diane Quinlan, Reg Brown*

Reg Brown bought the *Smoke* from Rothesay in 1948, an old gaff-rigger noted for its light air performance. She was "Queen of the Fleet" at the RKYC in 1949. Reg took the lead out of the keel and replaced it with concrete. A consortium of Danny Coles, Graham Logan, Bill Chisholm and Bill Conley bought her for fifty dollars each and had a good time with her for a few years. She finally ended up on the beach at Martinon to provide wood for bonfires.

Reg had the *Manana*, a narrow-beamed Cape Island boat on the cruise of 1950. She was quite fast and managed to have a collision with the *Tanya Dawn* of the Laskies, who said four planks were stove in. It was a basic trip. The *Don*, a National One Design, had a pup-tent over the boom, a small collapsible sterno stove and a thunder jug as amenities. Food consisted of hot dogs, soup, beans and sandwiches plus sporadic invitations to eat out. Sleeping on the floor boards was not uncomfortable but it was difficult to roll over with the centerboard thwart over one's legs. Moose McGowan, at six-foot-five, and Murray Sargent, at six-foot-two, were no more comfortable in the fourteen-foot dinghy, *Nonem*. Some improvement existed on the Lightning, *Malesh*, which had a spinnaker over the boom for cover to keep the American consul's son, Paul Miller, and Tony Oland dry. The *Cynthia*, a beautiful mahogany Bluenose class, with Dick Streeter and young "Doc" Petrie, was better yet. The cruise sailed from Douglas Harbour to Newcastle Creek, where an open air dance was attended and there were a couple of problems concerning local lassies.

"Pappy" Crumb was there with sons, Rod and Roy, on the beamy catboat, *Crumpet*, which was about eighteen feet long with a tarp for cover. They called her *Ex Lax* because she was good on the run. She was later raced by Dave McKinney and sold to Acamac, where Pat McBride and Audrey Sherwood found her and, in preparation for launch, sanded all that rough, protruding caulking cotton out of her. They had an awful time keeping her afloat. Blair Gould took her to Montreal and sailed on Lake St. Louis. Mr. Crumb invited the young fellows aboard and introduced them to Dr. Johnson's Snake Oil, which may have been a euphemism for rum. It was a rough reach the next day with a good breeze and nasty line squall, through which Tony was in charge of the *Malesh*. The crew of the *Don* was fully occupied bailing, barely keeping the boat afloat in his bareness with his pants around his ankles. Everything was sodden when she reached harbour but, fortunately, the crew were invited aboard Russell McNamara's palatial new yacht *Siboney* to dry out and warm up. She was one of two new vessels constructed in Malcolm Logan's shed on Kennedy Street in 1949. Malcolm created the *Cygnet* for Russell Wheaton with teak and fine cabinet work. The price for the thirty-eight foot craft was nineteen thousand dollars which the builder considered exorbitant. While the *Cygnet* was waiting for launch, Russell Mac was planking in the *Siboney*.

William Holder, the sailmaker, was well into his eighties when he lived at the foot of Orange Street on Courtenay Bay. He walked up over the hill and down about a mile to and from work at the loft. The author lived next door and he didn't mind company as far as Saint John High School, although he was hard to keep up with. One of our discussions concerning a suit of sails that he was making for the *Don* had to do with the jib where I wanted a couple of battens installed. He was difficult to convince and insisted that corset stays were better. Even then, they were hard to find. Judge Earle Caughey had spearheaded a move in St. Andrews to form a National One Design fleet. Three or four were built when war upset the plan. The *Don* was sitting in a shed in St. Andrews in 1944, for one hundred dollars, complete with sails, the owner being overseas in the forces. A Mr. Corbet had one at Morrisdale and another was under construction there.

Reg Brown bought the *Sigma*, an old yawl with a reputation for speed in 1951. She had a slight dip in her shear, aft of the rudder post, but that did not slow her down. The *Me and Jim* was a ketch-rigged salmon boat, or maybe a whaler, which encountered

Gladys Bell's natural history canoe trip at MacDonald's Point wharf in 1954, with Dr. Ruth McLeese, a paddler, Gerry Peer and others aboard. The boat was about twenty-four feet and open except for a small cuddy forward which admitted one. It was a warm, calm day, but pouring rain made one wonder about the sanity of the nautators. The craft was sold to an American who wanted to move it to the Hudson River. He hired Reg Brown as pilot, navigator, and engineer, and they set out in the autumn. The voyage was interesting, with the usual rudder and motor problems. They also had to duck into Newport, R. I. to ride out a hurricane with one man in the cuddy and one outside in the storm. The craft did get to its new home in one piece along with its crew.

In 1952, Kenneth and Murray Whipple met with Bev Appleby on his porch at Martinon and talked about getting some of the many boats on the west of Grand Bay together to race. This was the beginning of the Martinon Yacht Club, three dollars for the skipper and two for the crew. The fee was a bargain. After all, at a quarterly meeting of the RKYC, in 1949, there was considerable resistance to raising the dues from twenty to twenty-five dollars. The proponents argued that the Royal Nova Scotia Yacht Squadron charged sixty. Walter Lord, the treasurer, was great at recruitment. The first race was staged from the lawn of Guy Stevens' home at Martinon, with the starting line through his salmon nets. The keelboats included Ted Hartshorn's *Rascal*; Bob Hartshorn's *Sagana*; Stewart Dobbin's *Spray*; George Parket's *Surf*; Ray Hagerman's *Aesca*; Bob Barton's *Moby Dick*; Bev Appleby had had the *Moose*, a Comet class, but moved to the *Ricklyn*, the converted *Djinn*; Walter Lord had the Teal class, *Wish L*, built by the DeLongs; the Sullivans, the *Don*; Jim Evans, the *Tempest*, a Lightning; Eldon Card, the *Cossack*; and Doug Weaver, the *Blue Streak*.

There was a sawed-off shotgun mounted on a plank to start. Bev thought it did not make enough noise and clamped a megaphone over the muzzle. The result was explosive. Sound signals are necessary evils, whistles, horns and guns being used. The RKYC had various cannons; one, donated by Mrs. Spurling, lasted for years. Then the Cruising Club of America presented one to the club. It became a favourite. However, it was not without fault. Used on the yacht club cruise for signals, on one occasion it dipped at "colours," blowing a good-sized hole in the after-deck of the *Selu*, commodore John Schermerhorn in command. On another cruise, it destroyed its tackle at morning colours, disappearing over the side in Jenkin's Cove never to be seen again, in spite of multiple underwater experts. The visual signal was the smoke from the black powder charge of the gun. Shells used to come from Fred J. Watts Hardware but were discontinued, and Mike Flewelling did the packing for a while. The gun was fired from the second floor window and was sometimes not projected far enough out, causing sporadic cases of serious deafness to the starter. The method was abandoned in favour of experimentation with various types of pressure horns.

Time allowances or handicaps have always been a problem, and were the first cause of dispute after the first race of the new Martinon Yacht Club. No matter how scientific, complicated or simple the method, no one seems satisfied, but enough must adapt to keep racing. The volumes of hot air generated over the subject would fill many sails.

The Martinon Yacht Club cruise was more formulated than some others. The vessels headed for the sand bar at Douglas Harbour and stayed there. One year, about 1961, when most boats were open with tarps, they decided to be different and go to Chipman. They looked so miserable, the local undertaker invited them into his parlours for a barbecue, which was thoroughly enjoyed. The ice cream sundaes at Palmer Brothers General Store were always a treat and are still a great memory. A lot of crib was, and still is, played.

Toward the end of the 1950s, synthetic sails appeared. The *Zephyr*, a Lightning, had the first set locally, finding them a great equalizer. The RKYC Members Day race of 1958 was open with a good breeze, and the *Zephyr* first to finish ahead of many larger craft.

Bill Stroud's Lightning, *Stardust*, was the first on the river to be built to Olin Stevens' lines and had been seen to place if conditions were right, as off Belyea's Point on the cruise of 1950. Mike Marcus brought a Flying Fifteen to the RKYC in the late 1950s, the first true planing hull in the area. The design by Uffa Fox had been popularized by the Duke of Edinburg's *Coweslip*. She was exciting sensational in a breeze, but planing hulls are like any other displacement vessel in no wind. In an endurance race at the time, Reg Brown was drifting in the dark on the *Sigma* between Long Island and Lower Musquash, snoozing between sips of rum. The Flying Fifteen would catch him in the puffs but would drop behind in the lulls and could not pass. Mike later brought in a Raven class, twenty-four-footer, designed in Boston, and one of the faster planing boats of its time. He had the *Cygnet* after Russell Wheaton. The *Cygnet* went to Kingston, and Mike went to Victoria. He was seen at the first CORK in 1969, where he was second out of sixty-three in OK Dinghies.

There is a variety of weather on the lower St. John but the prevailing of the summer is the sea breeze that fills in at eleven hundred hours. Northwesters appear with cold fronts once or twice a week. Hurricanes tend to burn out in the Bay of Fundy but storm trisails and spitfires have been used. Rick Flewelling, who has made a career of delivering yachts around the world, had a Freedom 40 in transit from Bermuda to South Africa a couple of years ago and made a diversion to Saint John. He broached and filled it off Westfield on the St. John and became a carpenter for the next couple of weeks, decking in the cockpit for the following leg.

Zetes was sailed by Jim Barnes in the 1930s, as well as his *Raven*. Harold Holder had *Zetes* in the 1940s, participating in the RKYC cruise to Fredericton in 1948, when he was commodore and was featured in a National Film Board movie about the St. John River. In the late 1950s, she was proceeding down Grand Bay at night, in a northwester and somehow got through the old cross river breakwater of the old South Bay Boom Company, which had two openings, one small aperture near shore on the west for the boom tender, and one, not too wide, in the middle for the tugs. She was found in the morning, high and almost dry, in the mud near the wreck of the old bay schooner, *Glen Holm*, at Comely Creek, with her sails still full and looking like a ghost ship, with no sign of life. It was Sunday morning and the crew may have gone to church. How she got there and how she got off is a mystery. In 1960, when owned by W. S. (Tony) Taylor, moored at the RKYC, *Zetes* blew up, killing Mr. Philip Golding. Bill Nase was standing at the top of Millidge Avenue, near St. Clement's Church, when it happened and said the cabin went up to his eye level, which would be a good two hundred feet. The accident is thought to have resulted from gasoline in the water tank and a pilot-lighted stove. Though burned to the water line, there was enough left to reconstruct, which was done by Richardsons, as the *Lady K.*, forty-seven feet, and a distinguished racer under Mr. Douglas Kirby. She was a competitor in Monhegan Island, Marblehead to Halifax, and Bermuda Races. At the start of a Digby Race in thick fog, she was last seen heading into the ledges extending into the harbour mouth from Partridge Island, with Doug shouting "full astern," until she was spotted, tied up in Digby. Doug took her to winter in the Caribbean for several years and eventually sold her in St. Lucy.

Lightning, Zephyr, *Sullivans*
Built by Richardsons

The Lightning class, designed by Olin Stevens, made its debut on the river in the late 1940s. Two were built in West Saint John, the *Malesh* and the *Tempest*, but appeared to have a sag in the middle. They were faster than most boats their size, however. It was said that they had been stored for several years on a horse at each end. The *Stardust*, of Bill Stroud and *Betcha*, of Tom Chesworth Sr., were closer to Stevens' lines and really beat up on the competition. The Lightning could, relatively easily, be put together in a garage or basement. Ken and Murray Whipple each finished one, along with Les Rolston, *Bebe*; Cyril Brannen, *Dawncy*; Andy Oulton, *Whistler*; and George Foster. Ken Whipple did a second, fibreglass-coated one, *Scepter*, and Richardsons completed *Zephyr* for the Sullivans. *Zephyr* and *Scepter* had the advantages of synthetic (Teryline) sails from the start and were soon copied. Esteys bought the *Malesh* and then the *Stardust* and Ben Wade for another. The fleet numbered fourteen at one point and championship series were held for several years for the Lightning Bolt Trophy. Most had tarps fitted to go over the book by Holder's loft and with strips of plywood adjacent the centerboard box and on the floor in the bow, could be cruised by two to four people.

About 1961, Josh Bramwell acquired jigs for the Thunderbirds, twenty-six feet, which were faster and more comfortable cruisers. He went to work on one, followed by Murray Whipple. These proved so pleasing that next were the Bardsleys, *Mad Hatter*, Bev Appleby; *Birla*, Cyril Brannan; *Dawncy*, Ray Allen; and George Foster, using the WEST system. Again there were enough around to have annual one-design regattas. George Foster's was innovative and probably the best performer, but Bev Appleby was always at or near the top but was consistent at popping masts in all his yachts.

In the mid 1950s, Reg Brown moved to British Columbia, where he lived in the back of a car like the dinghy sailors of the

1970s and 1980s. He had bought a Tancook schooner, the *White Clover*, open and ballasted with beach stones, which he navigated from Mahone Bay. Over the next ten years, he added a cabin, changed her from schooner to ketch to yawl to cutter, depending on the handicap advantage. She won several Digby Races and ended up with Dougald MacKenzie, who took her back to Nova Scotia.

A vessel was stored and launched every spring at the RKYC. It would fill with water to the gunwhales and sit at her mooring in this condition until hauled in autumn. It was a Chesapeake Bay Sharpie, owned by an American. Reg paid an economical price and found good wood under the old paint with a fairly new Evinrude 9.9, in perfect condition, included. She was flat bottomed, with a centerboard, a cat schooner rig, and rotating, unstayed masts. The cabin had four berths, a couple of shelves and lockers with a cabin height of only about four feet. However, she may have been the original "pop top," as the roof could be elevated on four pieces of heavy duty studding by two feet, surrounded with canvas and screening. She was raced and cruised with trips up river and down the Main coast to the Cow's Yard, Rogue Island and around Penobscot Bay. She lasted into the 1970s, to be disposed of, still unnamed.

The *Barracouta* next arrived in Reggie's care, a Herschoff 38, which a syndicate had imported in the 1930s to beat the *Sigma* and stored in a shed in St. Andrews for thirty-odd years. She was the last wooden boat to compete with, and beat, the new fibreglass machines of the 1970s. However, age took its toll. Racing through the rips off Partridge Island, flying gibes in line squalls, and collisions at starting lines caused very troublesome leaking. She was sold, first to Nova Scotia, and then to a heritage museum in Connecticut, where she was beautifully restored.

In the spring of 1982, a disastrous fire swept through the two boat sheds at Colonel Holder's yard, destroying thirteen yachts and damaging several more. The Colonel's *Savitar* was built in 1895 at Quincy, Massachusetts, from southern pine and American oak. He had recently modernized the rig, changing from gaff to jib headed main, and stepping an aluminum spar in the thirty-two footer.

The Borrensen Dragon, *Flight*, of Brian Perry, also burned, as well the old campaigner, *Surf*, of Greg Dougherty. Others were *Banreigh*, Dr. Barry Beckett, the old Micmac Class; *Migsie*, Lyle Dyer, another Micmac; *Chado*, Perry Hutchinson; *Seamist*, Brian Marley; *Thetis*, Chris Belyea; *Loon*, Esmond Harvey; *Dovekie*, John Ferris, another antique; *Micmac*, Fred Page; *Ricklyn*, ex *Djinn*; *Jeep*, an old Micmac; and *Vagabond*.

Jollyboat, Hangover

Jollyboat, Hangover

Reg also brought the *Kristina* around from Halifax with Dr. Stephen Weyman, who made good use of her for several years. She was an English Robb design, wood, and about thirty-five feet.

Two other vessels came from Richardsons' yard in 1960-61, the *Ardessa* for Russell Wheaton and *Sura*, for Al Trafton. These were motor sailors of fine quality. Russell went to Virgin Gorda in retirement for a few years where he lived on her at marina, sitting in the sun and not sailing much. Doug Kirby visited and they put the canvas to her. Russell was on the wheel, having himself an enjoyable time, when Doug asked him to come below. The water level was halfway up the berths. Russell later sold her to Kingston and got an air-conditioned trailer in Corpus Christi.

Al was a great conversationalist and story-teller, enjoying the *Sura* thoroughly. He was on the top of Poley Mountain, skiing, when he had a heart attack, in the 1960s. He skied down the mountain on his own and went off, seeking medical attention. He had no problems after for over fifteen years, until he dropped in the companionway. His son, Aaron and wife, Bina continue to keep *Sura* in pristine condition.

These yachts were about forty feet, and John Fawcett was in the process of ordering another, when Richardsons were shut down. It seemed a shame that this should happen to an old, established firm when the government was financing a concrete boat works nearby at Chamcook.

Another interesting yacht at the time was the *Atlanta* which was Stockholm-built, from about 1898. She was well made and made the voyage from Estonia in 1948, overloaded with refugees. Her length was eighty feet, and draft thirteen feet, making her a bit large for the river. Charles Wilson kept her at the dry dock and Neill McKelvey took her in the Digby race of 1952, where the sails disintegrated in the gale. She went back into storage at the dock until acquired by Don Hartt of the lumber company. He did a major upgrade including new spars and sails but a quirky problem with the engine remained; it became disabled by the influx of sea water if the proper valves were not closed when under sail, and opened again when not. Her trips upriver usually were restricted to below Oak Point, being used more offshore. She encountered a fall storm on the way to the Caribbean, losing her sails and engine power, and the crew were removed by the U. S. Coast Guard. She was located, still abandoned, a couple of weeks later and was towed into Halifax by the Coast Guard. Her destination of St. Lucy was eventually reached for winter retirement and subsequent sale. An Estonian group bought her and returned her to Toronto with her bones now reported to be in Kingston.

Fred Brock of Rothesay brought in the *Titia*, the English 6 Meter representative at the Helsinki Olympics of 1952. She was another of the last fast wooden boats and competed against Viking 28s, Northwind 29s, C and C 30s and 35s.

Mr. R. C. Stevenson encouraged racing at the Royal St. Lawrence Yacht Club, where there were fleets of Finns and Uffa Fox-designed Fireflies and Jollyboats. The LaBaule speed trials of 1952 were dominated by the Flying Dutchman, 505 and Jollyboats. The latter became active along the U. S. east coast, even in Kansas, Lake Okanagan and Montreal, where there were about thirty at the various clubs. The *Hangover* was obtained by Dr. Herm Sullivan and raced with multiple Royal Victoria Hospital nurses. In 1962, crewed by Peter Kirkby and Charlie K. Sullivan, she won the Canadian Jollyboat Association championship and was seventh in the North Americans. The boat came to Saint John in 1963, converted from a three man crew to two, with a trapeze for the Worlds in North Carolina. She was unusual, when first over the line in the Settlers race, Charlie Cobham, ninety-four, sitting on the clubhouse porch, said little boats that fast should not be allowed.

For 1965, Charlie K. Sullivan had a Flying Dutchman, molded plywood, from Wolfgang's boat works on Wind Mill Point, near Montreal, called *Wildfire*. The two planing craft were equal reaching and off the wind but the FD went to windward much quicker. *Hangover* was sold to Dick Emmerson in 1966 and replaced by the FD, *Paladin*, a Dubdam Dutch glass boat. The plywood hulls were stiffer and found to be necessary for world class competition. Even so, the two boats attended National, North American and World championships, as well as Pan Am and Olympic trials.

Flying Dutchman, Paladin*, Dr. H. Sullivan*

Fibreglass was said to be indestructible when it first appeared, but 22 rifle bullets, fired at samples, disproved that. The gelcoat still scratches, requiring a talented technician to match and repair, and collects barnacles without bottom paint. Cored hulls, used in most modern high tech boats to keep them light, soak lots of water, which is usually detected by a moisture meter prior to sale and expensive to repair. In spite of these detractions, the material is the way to go, and wooden boats are hard to find. The Paceship *Eastwind* was displayed at the Montreal Boat Show of 1962 for four thousand nine hundred dollars. The price went up.

Fred Spinney imported the *Nordic* from the U. S. in 1961. Designed to be a rule beater, she was fast. Robert Logan obtained her in 1963 and raced extensively. The *Merry Major*, Cleve Belyea, and *Lady K.* were the main competition in A Class. In B Class were *Spindrift*, Tom McGloan; a twenty-four-foot sloop from the 1930s, *Zephyr*, Charlie K. Sullivan; *Banreigh*, Mac Somerville; *Crumpet*, Dave McKinney; *Don*, Bill Nase; *Dovekie*, Ron Gard; *Sally*, Ron Brown; and *Wee Scott*, Bill Hazen. In the Harbour Race of that year, Tom took the *Spindrift* inside the ledge at the southwest end of Mahogany Island, to gain a little advantage in the B Fleet. *Rascal*, Ted Hartschorn, was farther out and struck the rocks, propelling the bowman into the refreshing Fundy, but not for long. One wonders whether our savior trained here to walk on water. Mr. McGloan, who had the *Squall*, of Ingleside, in his youth, graduated to a Shark in the later 1960s. They would plane when the wind got up to fifteen or twenty knots and were very numerous in Central Canada. A fleet was racing at Rothesay Yacht Club at the time, with Bruce Tennant one of the better competitors. Tom had had a good Harbour Race in 1966. After having come up through the Falls, and above Pleasant Point, several motorboats passed, creating considerable wake and turbulence. Tom was standing in the lazarette, operating the motor and finding control unmanageable because of cavitation, when the *Rena M.*, fifty-two feet, which had been sold by Dr. Petrie to Toronto interests and the name changed, approached from astern. David Hartt, who was straddling the bowsprit, shouted to the helmsman to bare off but without response, and he came aboard, *T* boning the *Spoofin*, cleaning out the cockpit coaming, spearing Doug Gould on the end of the bowsprit, sending him over the side and into the water, and denuding the dorsum of the hands of Dr. Herm Sullivan, who swung under the bobstay, attempting to avert contact. With *Spoofin* rolled over and water over his knees, the captain commented, "We are sinking!" As the schooner backed off and the Shark rolled back upright, the helmsman of the former remarked, "That will teach you to tangle with the "Leprechaun"."

Good crew are hard to find and more difficult to keep. Dr. Gordon Mockler is a sport and natural athlete who had not tried sailing. He volunteered for the Rothesay Race of 1965, sailing on a Jollyboat, which had been compared to rolling off a log. The hiking strap broke, Gordie tumbled into the river in one direction, and the boat capsized in the other. He did the Endurance Race in a Flying Dutchman the following year, an air mattress having been added for his nocturnal comfort. Unfortunately, air mattresses and bodies, supine or prone, do not fit into the cockpit of a Flying Dutchman and Dr. Mockler sat up all night in a dead calm, snoring, against the starboard shroud. He gave another Rothesay Race a try in the autumn. While planing down the Kennebecasis in a good breeze, he was hanging from the trapeze, when a flock of ducks flew across the bow. Gord took a bead on the ducks and while he was diverted, the boat struck an unusually large wave and stopped. Gordie kept going and got wound around the forestay and into the jib. He was recovered but when examined, two days later, was contused on his port aspect, from neck to ankle. He has been seen at poker games since, but never on a sailboat.

The first fibreglass hulled sailboat was probably Joe Likely's Rebel Class, which raced at Martinon, antedating the RKYC's Flying Junior fleet. *Spoofin* and Neill McKelvey's Classic 31, *Quelle Vie*, were the glass cruising sailing vessels in the area. Neill's father, Fen, was a famous curler, representing N. B. at the Brier, and also, a harbour pilot. On bringing the pilot boat around from Courtney Bay one day in the 1930s, he struck an oar down off the sugar refinery and said, "There are the bones of the *Flying Cloud*." She was the renowned MacKay clipper from Boston that set the record of eighty-nine days to San Francisco, twice, which was not beaten until *Thursday's Child* in 1989. She was a coal hulk in Saint John Harbour in the 1920s until scuttled in the old ballast ground. Fen also took the *Duchess of Bedford*, a troop carrier known as one of the drunken duchesses, out of the dry dock during the war with a stiff south wind and foul tide. He could not swing her into the channel, so with the causeway to Partridge Island only about halfway there at the time, he ran her straight behind it. Probably not too many liners of her size have gone that way and definitely won't in the future. Post war, she became the Canadian Pacific *Empress of Canada*.

A few comments should be made concerning safety afloat. In the old days, the admonition was that everyone on a sailing craft be a swimmer and this has proved to be a good thing over the years. In the 1930s, Dr. George Skinner, eminent chest surgeon and contemporary and friend of Dr. Norman Bethune in Montreal, was a yachtsman. He was very conscious of the safety of his children around water and enforced the wearing of life vests. His son, Dr. Bernard, developed into an accomplished teacher and sailor in his own right, a member of Dr. Sandy MacDonald's Canadian Olympic 5.5 Meter crew in the 1964 Tokyo Games. After years of life-jackets, the offspring one day threw them in first before they dived. The flotation immediately went to the bottom like stones.

Dave Sullivan was about ten when he was sailing the *Don* on Grand Bay in 1951. It was the first year of a pilot study by the RCMP on water craft safety inspection, patrolling in a sixteen-foot Peterborough cedar strip outboard. Dave's rescue equipment consisted of a bucket, which acted as both bailer and life preserver. He was told that this was insufficient and to take down his sails and go home.

There were sporadic drownings, mainly when centerboard boats or canoes flipped and the occupants tried to swim to shore. It is still better to stay with the craft until help arrives. Up until the 1960s, there was little self-rescuing, and boats had to be towed ashore to be emptied. A hazard at night was the tugboat. Davis Patriquen was lost in his dinghy in the early 1950s. He passed astern of the tug but ran into the line and was run over by the unlit scows in tow.

Tugs were not all bad. On a warm, sunny afternoon with adverse wind or calm, one could drop a book into a log boom, making one or two knots, take off the sails and have a snooze.

In 1980, at the beginning of the Rothesay Race, with only a trace of wind, the *Myah*, C & C 33, was drifting below Starr's Island, trying to keep out of the down-tide, when an inverted outboard motor-powered, cathedral-hulled vessel was observed. Several other craft were nearby picking up those in the water, and a race was on, so the yacht materially-prejudiced rule did not apply. Two days later, Grenville Ring was encountered. He said, "Your father would never have done a thing like that! You left me there to die. You left me there to drown." Being nonplussed, the likeable elder relative was consulted about decorum and replied, "I would have thrown him an anchor."

Motorboats speeding after dark are the origin of many accidents. Thirty years ago, the Lightning, *Zephyr*, was rammed from astern, and the transom and afterdeck were torn up. The motorboat sank, and the occupants were taken aboard the sailboat.

At Acamac in 1998, a motorboat, the driver of which thought he was headed to the Ketepec Marina two miles away, hit a moored Kirby 25, destroying the transom, afterdeck, and rudder, and sinking the motorboat. The passengers waded ashore. The moored vessel was empty.

On a beautiful Sunday morning, as the cruise was moving up the Reach at ten hundred hours, an American forty-footer was proceeding up Chubb Channel. Early on in a proposed world cruise, the American boat was overtaken from behind by a high powered motorboat, which put a hole in his transom and catapulted the powerboat crew into the cockpit of the leading vessel.

Another daylight incident happened in the Jemseg River a few years ago when a runabout struck a moored Tanzer 22, while the crew were cooking supper. This was fatal to one of the Tanzer boys.

Lightning storms are not uncommon on the St. John, but serious damage to sailing vessels is. Most yachts are well-grounded by the mast protruding through the hull to step on the keel, but more attention is for those mounted on deck tabernacles, heavy cable attached, which goes through to the keel bolts. Incidents of damage to masthead instruments happen on occasion and it is nice to be near a craft with a taller mast, through which lightning it is hoped will discharge preferentially. One serious episode occurred in the late 1990s, when Mr. David Peacock's Corbin 39 was moored in Douglas Harbour. The owners were returning from Fredericton to Saint John. Deciding to drop by the boat to have a bite to eat, the owners found her sitting on the bottom. This was due to something in the order of eighty-three holes in the hull from a lightning strike. Repairs were accomplished and the craft is still sailing.

Fire has been a frequent cause of yacht destruction, tending to be more in motor boats. The *Gracie M* was burned in 1941 and *Zetes* in 1960. Motor cruisers included Roly Johnson's *Glooscap* and G. King Kelly's *Joan K* exploded in 1954 and 1959, respectively. The *Huntress*, built for Elmer Puddington and owned by Paul Hatty, went up near Oak Point in the late 1960s; Jack Logan's boat burned at her mooring, with Dr. Sean Keyes and boys, taking off the occupants to their Tanzer 22.

Birlia	Thunderbird	Flight
Bev Appleby	*George Foster*	*Charlie Kee*

Photo courtesy of Gary Pridham

There appear to be two main sources of blazes: fueling and cooking. Since the prevalence of diesel engines in the 1960s, there has been less danger because of the higher flash point. The possibility of fumes still requires a sniffer, either mechanical or nose. Speedboats seem to be susceptible to explosions after taking on gas. Dr. George Keddy was starting a trial runabout on a sunny, balmy, calm evening at Sandy Point in 1969, when the next thing he knew, he was standing in the river, his boat burned to the waterline, his hair gone, with his eyebrows and chest hair singed. Gary Golding had a similar experience when the first *Peaches* flamed in the fall at the RKYC wharf.

Cooking onboard can be hazardous, and alcohol stoves were preferred because water could be used to extinguish fire in that case. However, alcohol fires can be hard to see and follow. The stove on *Freydis* would leak, and fire would track down into the cabinet work, so it was replaced by a Coleman naptha unit, which could be heaved overboard if there was a problem. *Aquarius* had a small portable alcohol stove for heating coffee, as well as the larger permanently installed one. The little one overflowed and caught fire in the cabin one morning in Digby. The attempt to toss it over the side failed, tipping the alcohol supply bottle so that the cockpit became an inferno. Somehow, the conflagration was quelled but rattled nerves continued. In 1975, *Freydis* was on the inner sandbar at Douglas Harbour, with children on the sand and in the water, when Colie Wallace's powerboat, which had just gassed and was heading out the channel, flared with flames shooting out in all directions. As the blazing hulk appeared to be drifting back with the southerly wind, toward the pumps on the nearby wharf, the *Freydis* got underway and headed out the channel, encountering several people in the water who were taken aboard. Mr. Wallace's teen-aged son was quite badly burned, and was bandaged in homeward-bound fashion. Dr. Gardner, from Minto, who happened to be in the area, sent him to Fredericton for hospital admission. Later that year, while on the way down river, a houseboat was seen ablaze and adrift at Evandale, after refueling at the wharf.

Young people should have the opportunity to experience sailing to keep the sport vital. Mac Somerville encouraged junior instruction and pushed for the use of the RKYC Snipes for high school students in 1947, with some success. This move was followed at the Rothesay Yacht Club with the backing of Mike Marcus, Dr. Bernard Skinner, and Doug Parker. The plans for the twelve-foot Cadet had been published by *Yachting World*. It could be put together by an amateur, in a basement, garage, or living room. A program to provide a fleet of these craft commenced and, for adult involvement, the construction of a group of Rhodes Bantams was also included. Both projects thrived, although Dr. Skinner said junior training was great until the students got hold of the keys to the car. Doug Parker died suddenly at the finish line of a Rhodes Bantam race. Dr. Skinner went off to become a radiologist and Mr. Marcus went west. The program went dormant.

Renewed activity came at RKYC in 1962 when backing of Doug Kirby and the purchase of twelve fibreglass Flying Juniors, designed by Uffa Van Essen, and constructed at Mahone Bay by Paceship. This fourteen-foot class was raced around the world, with provincial and national championships attended by local sailors. Leonard Lee-White, of Rothesay, was the most frequent winner in this province.

The Mirror class dinghy, whose plans, like the Cadet, appeared in a British publication, the *Daily Mirror*, became popular in New Brunswick in the late 1960s and early 1970s with gasoline shortages and an increased preference for wind power. These dinghies could be car-topped to any body of water and were slightly larger and more beamy than the Cadet, making them suitable for adult racing. The kits were only three hundred dollars with sails and could be assembled at home. The *Mirror* has two mast step positions allowing a cat rig if preferred. All these training craft carried spinnakers except the Snipe. Out of these programs came the Nolts, with their *Lightning, Bristol 27*, and series of *Merissa*s; Dave Weyman, the Moulands and more McKelveys and Grants, Somervilles, Sullivans, Morgans, Hamiltons and Keyes.

In 1970, club racing changed. Glass boats such as the Paceship Eastwind 25, Westwind 24 and Acadia 30 with Tanzer 22, 26 and 28 models had emerged during the 1960s but were not dominant over existing designs. In 1970, the C and C designed Viking 28 from Ontario Yachts and Northwind 29 from Paceship arrived. The Viking was a kit boat with a skinned-out hull for home completion, while the Northwind was finished and quite amenable for cruising. They are both twenty-two feet on the water line, but Northwind has more beam and is listed at nine thousand five hundred pounds compared to seven thousand five hundred, giving the Viking an advantage in lighter airs. They proved surprising and exceptional for a couple of years. Larger C and Cs showed up: the 30, 33, 34, 35, 36, 38 and 40. Some more cruising oriented vessels also came on the scene, such as the Alberg 30 of Malcolm Somerville and 37 of Dr. Roger McKelvey; the CS 36, *Secoudin*, (Chief of the River) of Bill Nugent, and Cabot 36, *Patron Lady* of the Listers. Gerald Peer had a beautiful West system yacht, *Keloose*, built by Cover Boat Island Boat Works near Lunenburg, but he has recently gone to a glass vessel of the same name.

Ballad 30 class

Stormy, *G. Faloon;* Inferno, *D. Shaw;* Whistler, *A. Oulton;* Freydis, *H. Sullivan;* Abcana, *G. Cobham;* Excaliber, *R. Appleby*

Viking 28, Freydis

In 1969, the first Canada Games were held in Halifax. Sailing was included as a sport, and a qualifying regatta was organized for Shediac for the New Brunswick team. Norm Thurotte's three person crew, from Shediac, won the keel boat class in Westwinds; Bill Mouland crew, the FJs; and Bill DeNiverville, the single-handed. At Halifax, the keel boats were Solings, two person, FJs, and single-handed OK Dinghies, in which Bill DeNiverville won the gold medal for NB. The 1973 games at Burnaby had no sailing competition, but it was renewed in 1977. In 1968, Bruce Kirby of Ottawa, whose Kirby Mark 3 and 4 International 14 Dinghies had proved to be the world beaters, sketched the outlines of a proposed single-hander, which looked like the bottom half of an International 14. With the collaboration of Ian Bruce, of Physics 21 and engineering at McGill, and who was Prince of Wales Cup 14 champion, and Hans Fogh for sales, an entry to the America's Teacup Regatta evolved. It had a super debut at this event and orders showered in with ten thousand in the world very shortly. Peter Bjorne and Ward McKim, an Ottawa lawyer, joined the group to form Performance Yachts, subsequently produced Tasars, Lasers 2s, 470s and Laser 28s. The 1977 Games were staged at St. John's with sailing at the Royal Newfoundland Yacht Club in Manuels. Sail-offs were at Shediac for the keel boat in Mirage 24s, which a Martinon Yacht Club crew of Dr. Herm Sullivan, Bill Nase and Rick Appleby won. By this time, there was a Maritime Laser circuit with regattas attracting up to sixty-five entries. Based on performance in this circuit, the provincial team was selected, two over eighteen years, and two eighteen years or younger. These were MacGregor Grant, of RYC, Bill DeNiverville, of Shediac, Fred Kennedy and Steve Fleckenstein of RYC. The Games keel boat was to be a quarter-ton class, and the C and C 24 was selected. The NB quarter-tonners came home with a Bronze; Laser sailor Fred Kennedy, a Bronze; and Steve Fleckenstein, a Silver, placing NB third to Ontario and BC in points. Fleckenstein continued in Lasers and Finns, winning United Kingdom and US Laser Championships.

He also crewed the Canadian Star class entrant in the Pan American Games. Fred Kennedy continued in Finns and did well in U. S. competition. The 1981 games were at Thunder Bay with the Torrie boys, from Mactaquac Yacht Club, and Jamie Kennedy, RYC the representatives. Lightnings were the three person boat, and Lasers the other. At Saint John in 1985, Lasers and Laser 2s were selected with twenty-five and under and eighteen and under sailors in each class. David Regan, RYC, and Gary Sullivan, RKYC, did the Lasers; Andrew Brewer, RYC, and Charlie A. Sullivan, MYC, the twenty-five and under Laser 2; and Boo Davis and Campbell of Mactaquac YC, the eighteen and under. The competitors have been good but medals absent in the past twenty years.

The RKYC also hosted Y.O.T.S., a national event in 1985 with the Laser, Laser 2, and Mistral board, and Sail East twice in recent years with the Laser, Laser 2, 470, and Optimist Pram.

Laser II

Laser

Malcolm R. Baxter ran and had become president of Baxter Dairies, the family business. He had been brought up delivering milk at four in the morning from an early age and in the 1970s, someone told him he was stressed out and should get a sail boat to relax. Shortly, he had a C and C 27 and went racing with a good crew. He moved to a 36 for the Marblehead to Halifax Race of 1979. The *Knorr*, Peter Nickerson, and *Abcana*, Gordon Cobham, had competed in the 1977 version. *Charisma* was third on elapsed for her class, making the crew eager to do more. Mac went on to one of the first C and C 40s in 1980, taking her to the Monhegan Island Race at Portland and continuing across to Chester for Race Week, doing quite well. In 1981, she came second overall in her division, ahead of two other C and C 40s. After various discussions, Mac purchased a new, one-off, skinned out, C and C 41 racer cruiser which did the Gulf of Maine Series and Chester in 1982. It was selected for the Canadian Admiral's Cup Team, racing off the Isle of Eight, including the Fastnet with a C and C 44, another 41 and a 37 from Ontario.

At the same time, the RKYC renewed attempts to race for the Coronation Cup, which is still in NS, with annual competitions under the Universal Rule. It was even suggested that Mr. A. Walker, the owner of the sixty-five foot *Hayseed*, the Universal boat from Halifax, might join the RKYC, but the custodians would not budge.

The bicentenary of the settlement in Saint John of the Loyalists in 1783 and the incorporation in 1785 was at hand. A race from Halifax to Saint John, to follow the Marblehead, was promoted. In 1983, there was unusual interest in the Marblehead event, with twelve Saint John vessels participating. Herb Mitton's *Sugar* got a third and Bill Nugent's *Secoudin* a second, in their respective divisions. Sixteen yachts entered the race to Saint John in three divisions, with the fifty-five foot U.S. sloop, *Toscana*, the overall winner. In 1985, another Halifax to Saint John Race was run, with *Toscana*, again, victorious. On both occasions, the receptions in Saint John were magnificent.

Mac Baxter, Larry Creaser, Herm Sullivan, onboard the Charisma

In the Endurance Race of 1977, Bill Nase's *Jenn*, a Viking 28, had run downwind, along the Mistake, with *Barracouta* and reached the upper end of Spoon Island. She was in a gaggle of boats with *Nordic*, a C&C 30, and *Inferno*, a Paceship 29K, inside next to the island and *Merissa*, another C&C 30, outside, all of which drew close to a foot more water than the Viking 28, when the *Jenn* struck suddenly, while the other craft sped on by. Bob Harrity and his friend Brian, who were trolling off the stern, immediately pitched overboard where they found themselves in good position on the sandbar, to maneuver the boat back into the race.

Bob and I were delivering the new *Charisma* C&C 41 from Portland after the Monhegan Island Race, to Chester for Race Week in 1982, when we were stopped by a U.S. Coast Guard cutter at the Hauge Line. The crew were at the rails with their weapons but, after some polite conversation, we were not boarded and allowed to continue. It was the only time we beheld such armament aimed in our direction. Bob has been commodore of the RKYC since and runs a yacht brokerage, beside racing boats, Hobie 33s, and a J 36s called *Boss Lady*.

Bob Colpitts sailed for Canada in the Helsinki World Half-Ton Regatta with Vlad Plavsic, in the early 1970s, afterwards crossing the Atlantic in a Half-Ton Scampi 30 with his family. He is one of the few who tried wintering on a yacht, *Sweet Weather*, thirty-eight feet and center cockpit, in the climate of the Saint John Marina. It was reported as cold. Charlie Cobham tried it at the RKYC before World War II but had chickens aboard to keep him warm. A better solution was the *Lovely Lady*, a forty-foot motor yacht at the Saint John Power Boat Club. She was built out of mahogany by Richardsons in 1957 to Heber's plans, slightly modified by John Alden, for a retired American military officer. The newer owner lived year-round on her for some time.

Jim McDonald is another who has raced, navigated and administered with Mac Baxter on his many yachts. He has been commodore at the RKYC as well as racing and cruising his own C&C 36, 40 and 44, *Break Aweigh*.

Barracouta, *Reg Brown Jr.*

Start Marblehead to Halifax Race 1983
Panache RKYC C&C38, Peter Nickerson
Rhodes 19, Audrey Sherwood

Finish Halifax to Saint John Race 1983
Myah, *C&C33, H. Sullivan*
Sugar, *C&C34, H. Mitton*

In 1984, two J 35 racer cruisers arrived at RKYC, *Windancer*, of Gary Faloon, and Dr. Herm Sullivan's *Sumroo*, named after an Indian princess who contested foreign rule. These boats hammered each other for several years and were followed by a series of other light displacement sleds. Enough Kirby 25s and 30s were around in the 1980s for one design class racing. Reg Brown, having gone to fibreglass, competed in the 25, *Hornet* and 30, *Pharlap*.

North American J 35 Championships, 1984, Portland

Bill Nase, Herm Sullivan, Reg Brown Jr.

Kirby 25, Hornet, *Reg Brown Jr.*

C&C 40 Wolf, *Bill Foley*

J 35, Sumroo, *H. Sullivan*

Since the advent of electronic boxes, the Bay of Fundy fog and sea monsters have become less awesome with group and individual cruises along the east coast quite usual. The Royal Yacht Britannia was here for this one.

The Royal Yacht Britannia

C&C25, Aquarius, *Pat McBride; C&C33,* Myah, *H. Sullivan*

Myah *Off the Wolves, 1981*

J 30, Dulcinea, *H. G. Sullivan, H. Connor Sullivan, Colleen Sullivan*

Pat McBride's Aquarius, *brought in by Ray Allen and owned in between by Mike Flewwelling, a C&C 25*

Wayne Fulton's Hughes 38, Tara V, *from Halifax, underway*

Velos, *Dr. Leonard I. Morgan's Cross trimaran in Head Harbour Passage*

Fleet at Eastport with, right to left, Velos, Merissa II, Sumroo, Whisky Mac, Ultimate Investment, Kastle Rose *and two unidentified craft*

At Glenwood, left to right: Myah, *Herm Sullivan;* Windancer, *Kirby 30, Gary Faloon;* Daddy's Girl, *Ellis Levine;* Maria IV, *Mike Bruce;* Falcon X, *Gordon Cobham and David Green*

Phoenician Ark, *Hughes 40 of Dr. Anthony Boulos*

Long Island, with, left to right, centerboard sloop constructed by Doug Brown; Sumroo*;* Impulse*;* Mirage 27, Al Dodge

T.S. Ollabelle, *Sparkman and Stevens 47*

When summer has gone and winter's cold blasts arrive, what's to do? Ice boats were once boats with blades. Then, stripped down with a plank and two blades up front, a center platform and stern steerer, they evolved into streamlined bow steerers that can achieve speeds of one hundred-twenty to -thirty miles per hour. The plans for the DN 60, below, appeared in the *Detroit News* in 1938. It is the most numerous type in the world, cheap, easy to build at home, and car toppable. The hardware is available from Sarnes; speeds are in the sixty to seventy mile per hour bracket. There are usually a few on the St. John and Kennebecasis but the apex of popularity was in the 1930s. They require good ice, minimal snow, breezy wind, and the ability to be available when all factors are right.

DN 60 iceboat

Bruce (Moose) MacGowan, Bob Scott, Don Webster
Murray Sargent, Pat McBride, H. Sullivan, Barb MacGowan

Another vessel, which has been involved in racing, is the Millidgeville ferry in its versions, from the side wheeler, *Maggie Miller*, to the *Romeo and Juliette*. It is not that it wants to be but it appears like a lightning rod, particularly when its landing was at the end of Millidge Avenue. Doug Kirby and the *Lady K* used to often make it a target. It also obstructed on automobiles that drove down the street, off the ramp and parked under it. The pilot of the ferry once had the RCMP on the Peninsula side and the city police on Kennebecasis Drive and would land on neither. When its wheel house was changed from wood to steel, as the crane lifted the original off, there was a deluge bottle tops and tins from between the studding. Best of luck to the new boat.

Duck Hunting Appendix

Duck hunting has been a diversion around the St. John River since the arrival of Europeans, and conceivably before. A wide variety of ducks have made the area home or sojourned here. A selection of some of the species encountered over the years follows.

Surface feeding fowl tend to be native but also migrate as their territory freezes in the north. The American black duck (*anas rubripes*) is widespread, living in marshes and puddles, often remaining hidden until almost stepped upon. They then erupt vertically like a rocket and fly off horizontally. They are smart and learn about hunters quickly but will return to their favorite feeding areas. The Mallard (*anas platyrhynchos*) is a cousin of the black duck, has similar habits and interbreeds with them to the point of interference with the black's survival. Flocks of pintails (*anas acuta*) occasionally show up and decoy, and sporadic gadwallers arrive.

Teal are seen more often, swimming along grassy shores. Two varieties are native, the blue wing (*anas discors*) and green wing (*anas crecca*). The American widgeon (*anas americana*) is also a frequent inhabitant.

The wood duck nests in trees where box-type houses with a hole are placed by wildlife interests. Their plumage is much coveted by those who tie flies. Their take, however, is limited to one per day.

The lesser scaup, also known as blue bill (*aythya affinis*), is a well known native and also migrates through in large numbers. These are diving birds and not quite as good as the surface feeders.

The ring neck (*aythya collaris*) is a cousin of the blue bill and large numbers are banded locally as young birds in the Queenstown area. The greater scaup, or broad bill (*aythya marilla*), has apparently declined in population since the 1930s, with only the occasional bird retrieved these days.

Goldeneyes or whistlers (*bucephala clangula*) fly in from the north in mid to late October. Their wings make a distinctive sound and they are good eating when feeding up river but rather strong when down on the Fundy coast. Their cousin, the pretty little bufflehead, follows. They look like Yacky Doodle on the TV (*bucephala albeola*).

Shovelers (*anas clypeata*), canvasbacks (*aythya valisineria*) and redheads (*aythya americana*) are fairly uncommon. Common mergansers (*mergus merganser*) are nice to identify before firing because they taste fishy and most people will not eat them, although there is the odd testimonial to their splendid attributes. Old squaw (*clangula hyematas*) and scoters (*melanita nigra*) are found on the coast and taste like fish.

The double-crested cormorant, shag or hell diver is a great fisherman, loves eels and gets called a black duck more than any other bird, but is a useless nuisance and maybe should be shot for this reason. In China, a collar is put around a cormorant's neck so it won't swallow the catch when used for fishing.

The coot (*fulica americana*) is a smaller black diving bird that inhabits marshes, is slow to take off and often gets shot. There is not much meat on it, but a recipe for coot stew was in the local paper a few years ago.

There is a moderately large population of Canada geese that spends the autumn on the lower river. They rarely decoy and are seldom shot, except by accident. However, there are a few corn fields where they land, and success has been had. The late Dr. Carl Trask Jr. set up a goose pit, as done on the prairies, at Grassy Island in the 1960s, with over one hundred decoys. He had exceptional hunting that fall, until a local cow fell into the pit, could not get out, and died. The owners threatened to post the island, so this approach to hunting was discontinued.

Hunting ducks is not really a fair sport, and explanations of why it is done should be presented. It is a situation where the duck, with its bird brain, the quarry, has to outwit the hunter (*homus boobus*). Imitation ducks, wooden or plastic, are used to lure the quarry within range of the guns, the operators of which often act as if they were Bofors or 88s. The 12 gauge shotgun is only dangerous within fifty yards, but spent shot frequently rattles off one's hat. The bowman of a canoe has received a blast full in the chest, with bullets bouncing off his glasses and chest, fired horizontally across the marsh by a disaffected-nimrod. The duck's conception of size is limited so that over-sized dekes can be set. The epitome is that which contains the hunters and their equipment, with a hatch to be thrown open when the quarry is in position. Live decoys with clipped wings were in use until the 1930s. These worked well with a 6 gauge gun, mounted like a cannon, on the bow. The aspirants, camouflaged to varying degrees, hide in blinds of bush and netting, either on firm ground or surrounding a boat, canoe, or duckboat. Double-barreled guns are still in action but pump guns and automatics with six round magazines became available, allowing a tremendous barrage. Magazines at present are restricted to two shells.

The pursuit of the sport is said to be the result of heredity, love of the outdoors and nature, a need to cull the herd, the Von Richthofen complex, the need to work one's retriever, or even the need to kill. Sunday is a non-hunting day in N.B. and there is none before thirty minutes of sunrise, or after sunset. The season was once unlimited and started September 15 until the war. It now opens October 1.

The log of J. Fraser Gregory's yacht, *Zuleika*, for the trip in September, 1907, gives a fine description of how to go about hunting in a genteel fashion. The papers are courtesy of Thomas Chesworth and come from his family.

The *Senator* and *Foam* had more modest trips in the 1910s and 1920s but evidence of more ducks. There was usually a canoe or duckboat atop the cabin and one in tow.

Shooting Trip

Leaving Millidgeville at noon
on Thursday the 19th September
1907
on steam yacht *Zuleika*

The party on board were as follows:-

J. Fraser Gregory, Captain
Mrs. F. E. Williams, Mate
F. E. Williams, Cuban Consul, Boatswain
Mrs. J. Fraser Gregory, Chief Stewardess
Mrs. Rutherford, Chef
Mrs. Winters, supercargo from Chicago
Howard McCoy, Engineer

LOG
of the yacht
ZULEIKA

Sept. 16th to Sept. 19th

1906

THE Hunting Trip of the Season
  by Steam Yacht Zuleika
        leaving Millidgeville at 11 A.M. Sunday
            September 16th, 1906.

The WHOLE PARTY:-
  J. Fraser Gregory, Captain.
  F. E. Williams, First Mate and Crew.
  Jack Garey, 1st, 2nd & 3rd Engineers also Fireman.
  G. Colwell, Guide and general Supernumerary.
  The LADIES (without whom the trip would have been impossible)

  Mrs. Clement Rutherford & Mrs. C. A. Gray
  Jointly in charge of the Inner Man and the Ship's stores, whose duties included that of Cook, Stewardess, etc., etc., etc.

When leaving Millidgeville the water was as calm as a mill pond and as the Yacht left her moorings the sounds of "A Hunting we will go" from A. E. Prince's phonograph floated to us over the water while the crowd waved us a last farewell bringing tears to our eyes, but this was soon forgotten for off the end of Kennebecasis Island three gulls were sighted in the water. The Captain claimed first chance to shoot but he failed to bring down his bird, the shot falling short.

Passed Westfield at 11.40 a.m., turned up the Reach with the water almost like glass, what little air there was being from the South-West and directly behind us.

In our passage we passed the Yachts "Windward", "Mona", "Louvena", "Amorel", "Vagabond", Mrs. Rutherford shouting to the crew of the last named that she would certainly bring back a brace of ducks. Commodore Thompson's "Scionda", flagship of the Fleet, lay at anchor just off Brown's Flats. Several Cranes were sighted on the Mistake.

The run by Oak Point was delightful. It was here we passed the Tug "G. K. King" with several scows in tow. Unfortunately the ladies could not enjoy this part of the scenery, being busily engaged preparing luncheon and true to the old adage that a "watched pot never boils" the tea kettle positively refused to, and it was not until off "Grassy Island" that luncheon was served, then the Captain took the wheel and Guide Colwell, who steered through the Reach, came aft and no sooner was he seated at the table than three whistles of the Yacht brought all to their feet to see who had been saluted. It proved to be the "Lolita" with Fleet Captain Gerow in command lying at Palmer's Wharf. At the foot of Spoon Island our Chief Engineer spied a crow on shore which he had a great longing to possess. With the Yacht running at full speed he fired but missed of course. At Wickham Wharf we passed the Steamer "Elaine", Captain Mabee in charge.

The run from there to the mouth of Washademoak Lake was three miles, here we turned out of the main River and the real beauties began. The Captain rushed frantically aft and assisted the ladies in clearing up the dishes so that they, too, might enjoy the beautiful scenery. As soon as possible they reached the Upper Deck, the Captain took the wheel and Guide Colwell stood at the bow with pole in hand. The engine was reduced to less than half speed and we proceeded up Colwell's Creek not wider than the length of the Yacht.

Mate Williams was ordered to load his gun and stand ready to shoot anything in sight. A "hell-diver" suddenly appeared on the port bow and instantly did we shout "shoot" but he was too slow for anything and when at last he did condescend to he was so sure he struck it that he ordered the Yacht stopped and the boats lowered but Guide Colwell expostulated.

At 3.15 p.m. we dropped anchor at the foot of Foshay's Lake, 47 miles from home. No sooner was the anchor down and the boats than the sports of the party, Guide Colwell and Mate Williams, with one hundred rounds of ammunition, were off like the wind to begin the slaughter. The Captain took the ladies for a paddle in the canoe, but unfortunately for them this could not last long as they had to return to prepare dinner. At 5.30 all was ready the Bill of Fare being:-

Grilled Lamb Cutlets
Irish Spuds in the Shell
Celery & Radishes
Blueberry Pie, Tea & Fruit

The enthusiastic hunters had returned, the Engineer, the only one who got anything, proudly pulled out of his pocket three dilapidated snipe. Mrs. Gray presided with honours at this meal during the progress of which Mate Williams enlarged on the slaughter he intended doing that evening.

Mate Williams, Guide Colwell and Chief Engineer did not wait to assist with the dishes but as soon as dinner was o'er made for the Happy Hunting Grounds and, even before the rest of the party had cleared up, the banging began and we in the Yacht felt sure that game was coming down thick and fast.

The Captain with the ladies went ashore, the landing being very difficult in the mud and long grass. A long tramp was taken and quite a number of ducks were sighted but positively refused to rest within shooting distance. When the last vestige of day-light was gone they returned to the Yacht and anxiously awaited the return of the REAL hunters. Imagine our disappointment when they, too, returned without a bird.

Everybody set to work to clean guns, blow up air-beds and make ready for the night, orders being given for all hands to be on deck at 4.30 a.m.

Mrs. Rutherford would never have been invited on the trip but that she assured the Captain that she did not snore half as badly as her hubbie and she still maintains that she never snores, if not, she certainly nearly chokes to death in her sleep. The Captain assures us that if he sighed it was only for the missing wife and loved ones at home but the rest of us thought it was wild ducks coming on board, no quiet ones either. Mate Williams slept as peacefully as a child and assured us in the morning that it was because he had dreamed of Mrs. Gray.

Monday 17th, September 1906

At 4.30 o'clock Guide Colwell poked his head in the Cabin and called "Frank, Frank, the daylight is breaking", which brought him and the Captain to their feet in quick order, immediately all was hustle and bustle. The Captain lit the fire in the galley and put the kettle on and getting quickly dressed the Cuban Consul served hot tea to the ladies in their berths and to the anxious hunters. Through all the din and turmoil the Engineer slept peacefully.

The Captain, Mate and Guide took the canoe and made a detour of all the ponds but not a bird was seen within shooting distance.

At 7.30 a.m. their wanderings brought them back to the Yacht but as the ladies were still in dishabille, they could not come on board so proceeded down the creek, still without luck although a few shots were fired at stray ducks overhead. The Captain expressed a desire to land and the Guide suggested a walk before breakfast to a nearby farmhouse, a brilliant idea that was approved. Strange as it may seem they got cream and did not have to pay for it, a quart can heaping full and running over, they were also presented with two beautiful wings for the ladies, then proceeded to the Yacht for breakfast and the cream Malta Vita and number of eggs consumed by the Captain knocked him out for the rest of the day.

At 9.30 a.m. we weighed anchor for Gagetown with the Captain at the wheel and the Mate and Guide on deck looking for shots as we proceeded down Colwell's Creek and around Musquash Islands.

At 10.40 a.m. we reached our destination and immediately went to the telephone office and called up the loved ones at home whom we were sure would be glad to hear of our safety and happiness.

After promenading the length of the village street, the Cuban Consul acting like a goat, we re-embarked for Upper Jemseg world renowned for its hot weather and potatoes.

On the voyage the Trinidad Grass-Widow secured a snapshot of the Captain on duty, she also got a picture of the Chaperone aiming at a cow on the shore under the guidance of the Captain.

 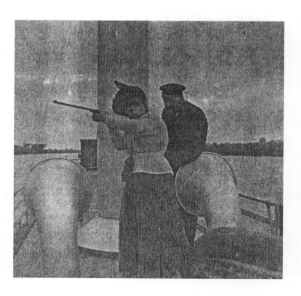

At high noon we tied up at Jemseg wharf for dinner. It being Guide Colwell's native heath he flew the coop to see his Aunt Maria and Mamma. At this point while waiting for the pot to boil the Captain made photos of the Yacht.

It was here the Chaperone displayed her ability as a marksman. After a couple or three shots at a target on the side of the wharf with a 32 rifle, she went up the road and challenged the village and we are glad to say that she maintained the credit of the party easily defeating the entire Colwell settlement, Mate Williams, the Chief Engineer and many Jemsegers and was presented with a plate of honey as a prize.

It was at dinner here that the Trinidad Widow disgraced herself, spilling gravy on the Cloth making a spot so large that it could not be covered with the pickle bottle.

At 2.30 p.m. we left for Grand Lake, a distance of two miles, the wind being very heavy we decided to drop anchor in the entrance besides the Captain was feeling ill.

Immediately the boats were lowered, the REAL hunters, with a lunch across the Mate's shoulders, got into the canoe and started out saying not to expect them until 9.00 p.m.

    In the meantime the artificial hunters enjoyed an afternoon siesta. The REAL Hunters paddled about two miles up Goose Creek as they entered the mouth a flock of black ducks arose. They LOOKED at them. They landed shouldered their guns and taking different directions each one tramped the long grass for miles on a pasty bottom but all to no purpose so returned to the canoe hungry and weary where the lunch so thoughtfully provided by the ladies was devoured, then again they took positions expecting ducks at sundown but again were doomed to disappointment, and for the Yacht. On the way they spied what they thought to be a duck in the water but what turned out to be a veritable Grand Lake Sea Serpent which made for the canoe with open mouth and tail in the air. It was shot by the Mate and after much effort dragged into the canoe and pounded to death with a paddle then shoved into the bottom. At last they sighted the welcome lights of the Yacht and as they drew alongside they told us of the tremendous monster they had caught. The stay-at homes rushed forth to their assistance with lanterns and ropes calling upon the Master of ceremonies to decide what the monster was and he declared it to be a Grand Lake Cusk caught out of season and ordered it thrown overboard.

    The Hunters had still to be fed although tea was over and the tables cleared, so the ladies once more got to work and prepared Meal No. 6 for the day. The appetites were enormous but the ladies did not consider it at all complimentary when, Mate Williams, in a spasm of laughter created by Guide Colwell, rushed outside and threw it "overboard".

    When the dishes were cleared up, Gun Cleaning again began on the Chaperone, with a swollen head on account of her expert shooting at Jemseg, declaring that she wanted a rifle for herself. Here endeth the second day.

During the 1930s, road and motor vehicle improvement permitted transport of water craft and equipment to various points along the river system more easily and rapidly. Then brackets were fitted on canoes. The pressure on the birds increased, was relieved during the war and then augmented by high-powered motors and speedboats. In hunting from a canoe, it is advisable to tie it to stakes in the blind. This was not done on a calm day at Grassy Island in early November, 1960. Even though it was a wide, flat-bottomed Chestnut Ogilvie model, when a solitary bird came at the decoys from abeam, the recoil from the bowman's shot put the craft upside down in about three feet of water, getting the sixty-four year old father in the stern very wet. Duck hunting finished and the bowman got the father's dry pants, while the old fellow kept his hip rubber boots and long underwear. An accident in the same era and area in a snow storm resulted in the drownings of Brad Gilbert and Jack Shuve.

A camper truck was acquired in the 1960s and opening day became a routine, usually parking at Queenstown wharf, but sometimes at Gladys Colwell's or John Day's on Colwell's Creek. The group would find room to sleep in the truck but split to go to blinds in upper or lower Musquash or in the pond holes of Long Island. Dr. J. K. Sullivan, who was several time Maritime Skeet champion and teamed with Dr. Forbes MacLeod to win the national doubles in the 1950s, slept in the upper berth. He was on the McGill boxing team with Dr. Vern Snow in the 1920s and his wife insisted on a separate bed because of his nocturnal sparring. His snoring was also legendary and he would say "I didn't sleep a wink all night," which was untrue, because no one else did.

In 1970, the *Freydis* was completed and made the voyage upriver for the opening. The year before, the water was high and upper Musquash had been sensational, although a Mountie almost drilled the old doctor while inspecting his gun. The *Freydis* was tied to a tree in the Killaboy Passage, the area inspected, and the decision made to return to upper Musquash, as the water was still higher than normal though not so much as the previous visit. Hay bales were taken out to sit on in a natural clump of bushes and another great opening day enjoyed.

Arnie Dobson, Ron Garnett

Restored Hinkley from Colwell's   *September 29, Arnie Surveying C172*

Dr. Bud Regan, Tom Chesworth, Dave Regan, Arnie Dobson, Ron

Herm Sullivan, Sophie

In 1966, the outboard was taken to Grassy Island in heavy rain and wind, where Dr. Gordon Mockler brought down two high-flying black ducks. It was then decided to check Rush Island, taking water over the bow in the rips off Oak Point. There was nothing doing on Rush, so the tour continued to the Isle of Pines to see how the doctors were making out there. The annual November 11 poker game, which began on November 9, was found in progress with governmental and industrial magnates involved at fairly high stakes. It was thought best to leave them undisturbed but the noble retriever ventured under the table and came out with his tail looking like the mark of Zorro, or Bingo, from the comic strip with Myrtle and Samson, who was always getting his tail caught in the screen door.

On the opening day of 1968, a calm, sunny, beautiful morning, Dr. Ken and Herman E. were settled in a blind at the upper end of Big Musquash Lake when Richard Belyea, in a nearby blind heard a shout, "Hey! Richard," who returned, "What? Herm?" Reply, "I think we're sinking." So Richard went to the rescue and there were the seventy-two and sixty-eight-year-olds standing in the canoe, up to their shoulders in water.

The 1971 excursion of the *Freydis* went back to the Killaboy. Conditions were drier and ducks were fewer. However, this opening coincided with an amphibious scheme from Gagetown, search lights on the wharves and elsewhere, rubber boats, ATVs and the Army's own brand of amphibious Ducks, sharing the river and marshes with their more usual occupants. Sleep was more upset than with the normal bird banding of the summer.

In 1972, the Killaboy was a hurricane hole. There were more birds in Big Musquash that year and two blinds were erected in storm winds and rain despite the absence of Arnie Dobson, who had been transferred to Bathurst. That afternoon, the boat's TV featured Canada vs. Czechoslovakia. The opening dawn was unique in that the number of surrounding blinds and artillery prevented a bird from approaching.

In 1973 and subsequently, the Hole in the Wall, or lead into Lower Musquash Lake, has been the destination. Ordinarily, the sail up has been very pleasant except in 1975, when the *Freydis* punched into a howling northeaster and rain, making no better than two knots on the Reach and taking ten hours to fetch Queenstown. It also rained the next three days. A Tonka heater was the ship's furnace.

The *Myah*, a C and C 33, draft six feet, replaced the Viking 28 *Freydis*, draft five feet, in 1979, which resulted in some obstruction to crossing the bar at the entrance to the Hole in the Wall, but seldom necessitated a tow. Until this time, there had been company in the creek, of ten to fifteen motorboats, mostly from Bobby Ring's yard, but after a disappointing shoot in the late 1970s, they preferred the lower river. At that point, the crew was Ron Garnett, Arnie Dobson and Dr. Gerald (Bud) Regan; and the area of Long Point was targeted for blinds. There were occasional incidents prior to the opening festivities, which included the loss of Donnie White in the marsh and then some of the party that went to the rescue. Another night, rest was interrupted as the motor boat, *Booze 'nd Snooze*, filled with water, slipping backward, downward and noisily into the creek.

A revival of Thanksgiving weekend hunting sprang up early in the 1980s, with hunters heading out on Friday night with the hope of shooting on Saturday morning and evening as well as Monday. The problem was that there were not many birds around by then, but more cruising yachts would arrive on Saturday to keep things in motion. Friday in 1982 commenced with a sail into a failing northwester, and power was applied at Brandy Point, then stopped when the propeller shaft broke; sailing recommenced. Evandale was achieved by midnight after two groundings and the loss of one crew to Morpheus. The two-horsepower tender was applied and when *Myah* was reboarded, no remaining souls were in sight. The craft coasted into the Hole in the Wall under main, and the hook dropped as the glow of dawn appeared on the eastern horizon. It was a hard morning in the blind.

Hole in the Wall, Sophie

An incident in 1978 accentuated the caution to be used around guns. Dr. Bud Regan was running the aluminum boat up the Otnabog in late November into a moderate north wind and temperature of minus ten Celsius. Spray flew everywhere and froze. The bowman loaded the Winchester Model 12 and stepped onto the beach behind the blind, at which time, the gun, coated with ice, slipped in his grip, dropping sharply downward. The grip stopped it as the hand hit the bead at the muzzle. The butt hit the frozen ground and the gun discharged. If the foresight bead had not stopped the slide, it is frightful to think of all that might have been lost.

An icy episode also happened December 12, 1984, near the end of the upriver season, with South Bay frozen and slush ice at the south end of Grand Bay. About forty black ducks had been spotted on Acamac Point the night before and dekes were put out for dawn. Shooting was good but retrieval depended on an old canoe of the 1920s noted for its instability. After using this method for a few birds, it was considered that it could be fatal. The next bird dropped in the dekes and retrieval was pursued in chest waders with a paddle, with the hunter disappearing except when bobbing for air. He got the bird but he looked like an ice cube and caught cold.

In 1984, opening day was carried out from a J 35 with a seven-foot draft which made entrance into the Hole in the Wall questionable, though an attempt is invariably made. One year, on September 29, an excellent solid grounding was accomplished with unsuccessful efforts to remove her by tows from bow, stern and masthead, and useless winching on the anchor. A Ranger and a Mountie stopped to check but said they had important things to do and took off with their forty horsepower. The bowline was winched tight to a tree on the island at the mouth to wait for high tide but she had not budged by morning and no one was clotheslined in the dark. The bow was tweaked around toward deep water with anchor, winch, and two hundred feet of line, where she moved.

C&C 38 Outrageous, *Rick Appleby, John Fallon*

Lately, the nimrods have had the benefit of what for better terminology might be called "referees". Mr. Bill Nase, Rick Appleby and John Fallon have been present on the *Outrageous*, looking after the ducks' interests and encouraging them while minding the hunters' nutrition. The roast beef has been exceptional.

The ducks were declared winners in 2000, on a bright, warm, sunny, calm morning, with the engineer, Tom Chesworth, sitting in the stern, eating an apple. The lookout, Robin Adair, was crouching in the bow, concentrating on a sandwich, when a lone bird attacked the decoys from abeam and out of the sun. The middle watch, standing on the rowing thwart, took aim, fired two shots, and found himself doing the backstroke in Musquash Lake. As he scrambled through the bush and the brambles to recover his position, the remaining occupants of the boat wondered where he went. As he appeared, Tom leaned to assist re-entry, and Robin rushed to the stern exclaiming "I'll help." The boat filled and sank. Someone advised that all should get in the boat. This proved that the boat was on the bottom, depth was three feet and that the flotation was insufficient. The next order was "Everyone out of the boat." After this was accomplished, bailing commenced, life jackets were donned and the craft was eventually and carefully reboarded. The motor was, of course, drowned, and the rowlocks did not fit, so paddling began. A young hunter from a neighboring site dropped over and offered a tow, saying, "I wondered if you were having a bit of trouble, but I didn't like to upset your hunt."

October 1; Bill Nase, Sophie

The ducks won again in 2001 and 2003 when the blind could not be located because of thick fog.

Sojourner, *Richard Belyea*

Off to the night shoot; Bill Nase and Herm Sullivan looking on

After the hunt.

Sophie

Robin

Tom, Pat, Herm

After the hunt, duck plucking

Herm in the boat; Tom in the mud

Index

ABOUT THE AUTHOR

A graduate of the McGill Medical School, Dr. Herman Sullivan practiced urology in Saint John for almost forty years. He got his first sailboat when he was four years old, and he's been sailing ever since. He's been listening to sailors' yarns (and has been part of many!) for over seventy years. *Gone to Yacht* is his first book.